Cat

Catholic Voices

*Putting the case for the Church in an era of
24-hour news*

Austen Ivereigh and Kathleen Griffin

DARTON · LONGMAN + TODD

First published in 2011 by
Darton, Longman and Todd Ltd
1 Spencer Court
140 – 142 Wandsworth High Street
London SW18 4JJ

ISBN: 978-0-232-52863-3

Phototypeset by Kerrypress Ltd, Luton, Bedfordshire
Printed and bound by CPI Antony Rowe, Chippenham

Contents

Foreword

In September 2010, Benedict XVI touched down at Edinburgh airport, the first Pope ever to come to the United Kingdom on a state visit. He was greeted by enthusiastic crowds and a small but media-savvy Protest the Pope campaign. As the first day of the visit drew to a close, one of their spokesmen appeared live on Sky News to put their case. It was my job to oppose this but I was not in the same studio as my opponent, so I had to listen to him through an earpiece. At the critical moment, the technology broke down and I could hear nothing. When the interviewer asked me to respond, I explained my problem but said that Protest the Pope always said the same thing so I could respond anyway. Taking my heart in my hands, I said that, regarding abusive priests, the Vatican only had files that were sent to them by local churches and hence they were not secret; no police force had ever approached the Vatican to ask for secret files. Rather than being part of the problem, I continued, it was Cardinal Ratzinger – now Pope Benedict – who had insisted that local bishops inform him of any abusive priests to ensure they were dealt with firmly. Finally, I noted that in his arrival address, the Pope had affirmed the great traditions of Britain that flowed from our Christian heritage.

It transpired that I had refuted all the arguments put forward by the Protest the Pope spokesman even though I had not heard a word that he said.

This book is the fruit of listening to the Catholic Church's critics and realising that they usually deploy the same arguments. There are coherent responses to these criticisms and this book offers such responses. Even more importantly, it shows how to approach these criticisms in a positive way, getting to the heart of what really concerns the critical questioner and not simply responding negatively. This art of reframing is wonderfully illustrated throughout the book. The Catholic Church has good news to pass on and must not let critics push Catholics into making the Gospel sound like bad news.

The Catholic community in Britain holds a special place in both the history of the country and the history of the Church. The Catholic Church is a minority community in Britain and has been for over 400 years; just seven per cent of the British population belong to it. Yet as part of the world's largest religious community of some 1.1 billion people, the Catholic Church in Britain can explain to this country the religious faith of approximately one-sixth of the world's population. As a minority, British Catholics have learnt how to explain themselves to their compatriots and in Catholic Voices this ability found fresh expression: young lay people ready and willing to take on the fast-paced medium of non-stop news. This skill is of benefit not only to the Church but to the wider world because faith communities are a vital and enduring part of our global society. The ability to understand religion is a key skill for modern life.

There was a widespread theory that as modernity spread around the globe religion would decline. The twenty-first century has already shown that this is not true. We live in a religious century, where the world's most modern country, the USA, remains strongly religious. Alongside this, the appalling misuse of religion has replaced the atheist philosophies of the twentieth century as the inspiration of some the world's cruellest political movements. Modernity has to come to terms with the durability of religious faith and the need to understand how to distinguish good religion from bad religion. So believers have a duty to explain themselves in simple, coherent terms to their often bewildered contemporaries.

This book is therefore not only for Catholics but for all those who wish to understand how the world's largest faith community explains itself in contemporary terms. The ability of Catholics to communicate the Church in relevant ways depends on firstly listening to contemporary criticisms and then responding appropriately. Similarly, to understand the Catholic faith, people need to listen with equal attention to the explanations.

So this book is an exercise in listening as well as in speaking. With good listening on all sides, our century can achieve a unique historical milestone in mutual understanding between the world's faith communities. This book is a significant contribution to that task. May all who read it enjoy a moment of Pentecost, that moment when the Holy Spirit enabled the disciples to be understood by those who did not speak their language.

Dom Christopher Jamison OSB
Patron, Catholic Voices

Acknowledgements

This book was born of a project involving many people caught up by a single idea: to make sure that Catholics and the Church were represented properly in the media when Pope Benedict came to visit the UK in September 2010. It was a project that needed co-ordinators, speakers, experts, patrons, a chaplain, an assistant, a media bids coordinator, and some generous backers. This book is the fruit of the commitment of all of them, and we offer it to them with deepest thanks.

Needless to say, the usual caveat applies: although it has benefited from input from others in the project, we take sole responsibility for its contents. Where it contains dazzling insights, these are likely to have been culled from the experts we grilled in the briefing sessions; but the flaws and inaccuracies are ours alone.

The authors are two of the project's three coordinators. Jack Valero, the third, has been at our side the whole way with his invaluable energy and enthusiasm, as has Eileen Cole. Michael Moore, originator of the 'positive intention' idea, has been invaluable. A big thank you to the experts who offered champagne for our brains, among them Clifford Longley, Ben Andradi, David Albert Jones, Fr Michael Czerny, Charles Wookey, David Quinn, Fr Andrew Pinsent, James Hannan, Dermot Grenham and Neil Addison; and of course to our media gurus: Colin Brazier, Bess Twiston-Davies and Stephen Cole.

Fr Stephen Wang, chaplain to Catholic Voices, has counselled and inspired us. The Catholic Voices board has advised and supported, as has Fr Christopher Jamison, a model 'CV', to whom we are indebted for the preface. Lord Brennan, CV's other patron, has grounded and networked us. Various bishops, not least Archbishop Vincent Nichols, and their staff at the Catholic Communications Network, especially Alexander DesForges, have encouraged us without ever interfering. And we thank Brendan Walsh, editor at Darton, Longman and Todd, and his team, for mother-henning this egg with skill, patience and humour.

But mostly we wanted to mention by name the first Catholic Voices speakers' team, who volunteered in March 2010 to be grilled by BBC and Sky presenters in 'as-live' interviews, and then, the following September, to go 'live-live' in studios across the land. They put their trust in us, and proved wonderfully that our vision of Catholic communication is possible.

So hats off to the brave pioneer Catholic Voices: Bonnie Lander Johnson, Chris Serpell, Laura Crowley, Christopher Morgan, Daniel Coughlan, Michael D'Arcy, Dominic Burbidge, Edward Rennie, Fiona Paley, Ella Leonard, Fiona O'Reilly, Fr Paul Keane, Jim Carr, Madeleine Teahan, Poppy MacDonald, Neil D'Aguiar, Marie Jones, Peter Williams, Patrick Cusworth, Robert Colquhoun, William Johnstone and Jim Carr – witnesses and light-spreaders all.

Introduction

We know how it feels, finding yourself suddenly appointed the spokesman for the Catholic Church while you're standing at a photocopier, swigging a drink at the pub, or when a dinner party suddenly freezes, and all eyes fix on you.

'You're a Catholic, aren't you?' someone says.

'Um, yes,' you confess, looking up nervously at what now looks like a lynch mob.

The Pope has been reported as saying something totally outrageous. Or the issue of AIDS and condoms has come up. Or contraception. Or that new thingy they've created to poach Anglicans. And here you are, called on to defend the Catholic Church by virtue of your baptism, feeling as equipped for that task as Daniel in the den of lions.

Go on, they don't actually say. Justify that.

Scrabbling together a few thoughts, you put up a valiant defence, and people nod sympathetically. You contextualise. You point out x and y, make a few observations they hadn't thought of, bring a little perspective into the question. The mob dissolves; people smile. They're not persuaded, but they don't want you to feel uncomfortable.

Or it didn't happen that way at all. What happened was you got a little flustered and said a whole load of things which sounded pretty unpersuasive – even to you. You got irritated at the Church being constantly made to answer to a self-appointed inquisition of secular humanists and accused of bizarre conspiracies by people who had read too much Dan Brown. In fact, you became flustered and flew off the handle; the feeling of persecution got to you. By the time you had spluttered out your angry defence, the gulf between you and everyone else had widened impossibly – and your host had quickly, nervously, introduced a new topic while passing the pudding.

Either way, here's what didn't happen. You didn't manage to 'reframe' the issue. People still had the same view of the Church – dogmatic, authoritarian, anti-democratic, hypocritical, inhuman – as before you started speaking. You didn't turn the tables, re-cast the issue, open minds and hearts. You were stuck inside your opponent's frame.

As we were saying, we sympathise. It's not easy, putting the Church's case. The issues are sometimes complex, and the headlines grotesquely simplistic. And it's hard to know sometimes what the Church's view actually is. Maybe you heard a bishop or theologian on the radio answering precisely that point. Maybe you've read up on it. But most likely, you just don't have the time to conduct major research on issues that keep coming up in conversations. You're bright and a committed Catholic. But you're also busy.

What you wish you had was an adviser, someone you could summon for a quick briefing, who could offer you (a) a bit of background, (b) a survey of the key issues, (c) some suggestions of how you might reframe the issue, and (d) some key points you could draw upon next time the question arises.

Well, here we are: not quite an adviser, but the next best thing – a book full of precisely such advice. Practical advice.

What you'll read in these pages is the result of a group of Catholics getting together to prepare themselves for precisely these high-pressure, get-to-the-heart-of-it-quick, kind of contexts: not just around the water-cooler, but in three-minute interviews on live television. Our experience is what enables you to 'reframe' the hot-button issues which keep coming up in the news and provoke heated discussion. We call these issues 'neuralgic' because they touch on nerve endings, those places in the body which, when pressed, cause people to squeal. In our public conversation, they are the points which lie on the borders where mainstream social thinking inhabits (at least apparently) a different universe from that of Catholics. Touch on them, and people get very annoyed. 'How on earth can you believe that?' they ask you.

This book doesn't tell you what to say. Every conversation is different. And it can't help you know what's coming up in the news on a given day: not even the people who make the news can predict that. But most news stories take place against a background of one of those neuralgic issues. This book helps you to think through those issues for yourself, to understand where the criticism is coming from, and to consider how to communicate the Church's positions on key questions in such a way that you do not accept the presuppositions of the criticism. At the end of each of the nine briefing chapters, there are some 'key messages' which summarise these positions – and which will help you next time you're challenged.

But first, a few words about the method and approach used here, where it comes from, and what we're hoping to achieve.

The book is named after the project which gave birth to it. Catholic Voices is a team of trained amateur speakers formed in advance of the visit of Pope Benedict XVI to the UK in September 2010. The team consisted of 'ordinary' Catholics – in other words, Catholics who had jobs and children and paid mortgages – who were happy to put across church positions and teaching on radio and TV in the run-up to and during the papal visit. They were advertised to the media as 'media-friendly, studio-ready and ego-free', by which we meant: happy to be questioned, and sympathetic to the media's objectives and *raison d'être*; familiar with the demands of three-minute live interviews, and the constraints and possibilities of radio and TV; and unselfconscious, happy to be used or not used as the situation demanded. We also described Catholic Voices as 'authoritative but not official': we set out to be well briefed and articulate, knowledgeable, and able to communicate the settled teachings of the Church. But while we had the blessing of the bishops, we did not speak for them. If you wanted to know how the bishops responded to such-and-such a story in today's news, you would need to call their spokespeople. But if you wanted to know what the Church believed and taught, you could call us.

At the back of the book we tell the Catholic Voices story, and hear from the CVs (as they became known) themselves what it was like in the weeks leading up to and during the papal visit.

But here's the headline: the programme was a success. They had around 100 media appearances (you can watch a selection at www.catholicvoices.org.uk) including dozens of debates with 'Protest the Pope' campaigners and other critics, and received praise from bishops and broadcasters alike. We were on all the major channels – BBC News 24, Radio 4, World Service, World TV, *News at Ten*, Five Live, *Newsnight*, regional radio and TV, Sky News, *Channel 4 News*, and so on – as well as many local and foreign new outlets. The project has led to us being asked to advise similar initiatives in other countries, set up by Catholics inspired by our example. In the UK, we received dozens of messages congratulating us and asking if there was a way of sharing the fruits of our training more widely: hence this book.

There have been many other fruits, including informal dialogues with humanists and abuse victims, a second speakers' training programme, and a new 'Academy' which can continue to develop ways of amplifying the voice of the Church in the public square.

But perhaps the most important fruit of the Catholic Voices experience was the 'method' we developed in those months: one that we think works for anyone who needs to put the Church's case, not just in a three-minute live TV interview, but also in a three-minute live pub conversation, or a half-hour lunch-break discussion provoked by an item on the news. After all, the two situations are not so different. If you can't say it quickly, compellingly and humanly, then you've lost people's interest and sympathy. That may not be a disaster. But it's certainly a missed opportunity.

What we learned was a particular mindset, one that helped us to avoid being defensive or aggressive, which was vital to enable us to 'reframe' the criticism. We've summed up that mindset in a series of principles, which overlap with each other, but may well be a means of reviving the art of apologetics for our age – an era of 24-hour news. Those principles – 'light, not heat'; 'people don't remember what you say as much as how you made them feel'; 'it's not about you', and so on – are listed separately at the back of this book, so you can look at them anytime you're about to enter an environment in which you'll be challenged.

At the heart of this mindset is what we call 'positive intention'. The idea is that behind every criticism of the Church, however apparently hostile or prejudiced, is an ethical value. The critic is consciously or unconsciously appealing to that value. Issues become neuralgic, in fact, precisely because those values are at stake. Surprisingly, perhaps, the value is one you might recognise as being valid – Christian, even; or at least derived from a Christian value.

That's not so astonishing, given that we live in Christian cultures, however secularised. What secularisation means is that people abandon the Church yet continue, unconsciously, to adhere to its values – and often appeal (again unconsciously) to those values when they criticise the Church. By realising the positive intention behind the criticism of the Church, it is much easier to persuade the critic, because your answer will be able to appeal to that same value. At the same time, you will be less defensive, because you're able to empathise with that value. Empathy is the beginning of dialogue. Dialogue does not mean abandoning or adjusting your values, but building relationships of trust between people of differing convictions. This book teaches the art of that dialogue: not how to defend positions, but to explain them, to enable others to understand them.

By looking at the positive intention behind the criticism we were able to get out of the mindset of 'how can I justify this?' and ask: 'what is the real source of the disagreement here?' To take an example: the desire for an assisted suicide law is based on the positive intention that people should be spared unnecessary suffering. Now we, as Catholics, agree that, while suffering is inevitable in ageing and dying, no one should experience unbearable pain and loneliness – which is why Catholics such as Dame Cicely Saunders created the hospice movement. So now that we can agree on that, we can then look at where we disagree – the meaning of death, the question of autonomy etc. – and then look at the practical issue of what an assisted suicide law would mean for health care, for the view of the elderly, and so on. The discussion can become more rational and constructive because we are not arguing with people from another planet but with people who are part of our same culture of values.

In each of the chapters, therefore, you'll find, early on, a box about the positive intention behind the criticism. It will help put you in the mindset of the critic – and realise that we have a job of explanation to do.

At the beginning of each chapter, you'll also see a list of 'challenging questions'. No one can predict exactly what questions will be asked about a particular neuralgic issue. News stories vary. Yet because the neuralgic issues remain constant, the questions are reasonably predictable. The Catholic Voices were amazed to find that the questions they faced in studios were almost always variations of the ones we had considered in the briefings. That's because the positive intention behind the criticism generates a series of natural questions. But don't think our challenging questions are in any way exhaustive. You'll easily add some of your own.

You'll also find, in the course of each chapter, allusions to documents and sources. We've tried to keep these to a minimum. And in order not to weigh the text down with footnotes, you'll find the references in each chapter explained and expanded on at a special section on our website, www.catholicvoices.org.uk/bookresources, where you'll also find many of the reports mentioned in the text, along with links and suggestions for further reading.

Before we leave you to the book, a quick word about scandal – and an invitation from Pope Benedict XVI.

The Catholic faith 'scandalises'. It causes people to react strongly and ask hard questions. Thank God for that. That's what the Gospel does. 'Blessed are they who are not scandalised by me', says Jesus, referring to those who do not turn away in disgust or incomprehension. But it's Jesus, of course, who lays down the stumbling blocks – the *skandala* as they're called in Greek. A *skandalon* is an obstacle in the path. It causes people to stop and think; their existing frame is threatened. And this can be the start of another path, one that leads, potentially, to a new way of looking at something. Or it can lead to the 'turning away' which Jesus warns of.

That turning away – that furious rejection – is the enemy of true communication. When people are troubled and ask questions – even if the questions are in the form of angry accusations – they have not yet turned away. That is why every radio and TV interview, every discussion over a beer, every frozen dinner-party moment is an opportunity. Is this evangelisation? We see it more as 'clearing the obstacles to evangelisation'. It's clarifying misunderstanding, shedding light where there is myth and confusion. It hopefully causes people to reconsider their objections to what the Church says. Whatever we want to call it – 'apologetics', 'communication' – it's a witness, and a vital one.

In media news terms, it's getting in at the beginning, to reframe the story as it's breaking. Some call this 'spin-doctoring', a term that's derived from cricket. The aim is to 'doctor' – to correct – the spin that the bowler (the news story, the critic) has put on it. The term is discredited, because it suggests the dark arts of media manipulation. That's why we prefer the term 'reframing'. It's not a disreputable or manipulative thing to do if what you are doing is telling the truth: reframing only works if what you're saying is true. 'False ideas may be refuted indeed by argument,' said Blessed Cardinal Newman, our lodestar in this enterprise, 'but by true ideas alone are they expelled.'

It's a witness. It's also a vocation. We're hoping that this book serves also as an invitation to 'ordinary' Catholics – that's probably you we're talking about here – to see themselves as communicators. Some people (again this may be you) have a natural gift for this. They are the kind of people who love to gnaw over an issue, or the kind of people who love to clarify and build bridges. There are many kinds of Catholic communicators: some delight in concepts, others speak out of experience; some are impassioned orators, others are gentle, thoughtful types. But they are all motivated by a desire to put across their faith in human, compelling ways. They are also a bit impatient – to get out there and correct some of the frustrating misapprehensions they hear every day about the Church they love.

This, as it happens, is eminently a mission for lay people, as Pope Benedict said in his homily at Bellahouston Park in Glasgow:

> I appeal in particular to you, the lay faithful, in accordance with your baptismal calling and mission, not only to be examples of faith in public, but also to put the case for the promotion of faith's wisdom and vision in the public forum. Society today needs clear voices which propose our right to live, not in a jungle of self-destructive and arbitrary freedoms, but in a society which works for the true welfare of its citizens and offers them guidance and protection in the face of their weakness and fragility. Do not be afraid to take up this service to your brothers and sisters, and to the future of your beloved nation.

It's a task far bigger than defending the Church's rights, or even the rights of faith; it's about being able to articulate what is, in fact, a treasure for all: the value of religious freedom, from which all other freedoms flow; an authentic pluralism which allows for a vigorous civil society, a community of communities – not just the state, market and atomised individuals. It's about being able to apply the great social encyclicals, using their open human language and concepts, to the needs and demands of Britain today – highlighting the needs of the poor and disadvantaged, calling for virtue in public life, and the building of institutions, and helping to define a better relationship between state, market and civil society. It's about advancing a vision of society which defends life – however feeble or invisible – and the dignity of every human being. It's about helping to build a civilisation of love.

Hence the need for Catholics who 'know their creed so well that they can give an account of it', in Newman's phrase. The public square is, to a very large extent, defined by the TV and radio studios. That's where the Courtyard of the Gentiles is, that's where the chatter of the *agora* is to be found; and it's where Catholics need to learn to be at home, speaking humanly, succinctly and compellingly of their Church's vision. But the public square is also where you are: where you interact with others, in the many crossroads of our contemporary society. If this book inspires you to get together with others to develop your ability to communicate the Church, we'll be delighted.

Actors and writers often talk about finding their voice – that moment when the character they've been working hard at creating comes alive and hits the right notes. That's something the Church always needs to do, in each generation: to find its voice in society. And it's something every Catholic is called to do – in the media, yes, but also in the workplace, among friends, and at those dinner parties which suddenly freeze over.

We hope this book helps you find your voice.

Part I

Chapter 1

The Church and politics

Challenging questions

- *Why does the Church interfere in politics — shouldn't it just keep to religion?*
- *Why does it try to control Catholics in the way that they vote — and to pressurise Catholic politicians on questions such as abortion?*
- *What right does the Church have to interfere in the laws of secular states?*
- *Is it a church or a state? Why does it act like a state?*

The idea that the Catholic Church 'interferes' with national sovereign politics is nothing new. Rulers (and voters) have always resented being held to account by a higher law. In the age of democracy, the accusation is sometimes levied against the Church that it acts as a kind of lobby, using its spiritual influence to engineer certain political outcomes – acting, in other words, out of corporate self-interest. Critics accuse the Church of 'imposing its view' on the rest of society, in an attempt to thwart human rights – usually understood narrowly and one-sidedly as those of a woman to seek an abortion, or a gay couple to adopt a child.

A specific neuralgic issue is the Vatican's status as a state, or rather, the international influence of the Holy

See, the seat of governance of the Church worldwide. In the weeks before Pope Benedict XVI's visit to the UK in September 2010, the 'Protest the Pope' coalition objected that, if the Pope was a faith leader, why was he being received as a state visitor? Surely, the protesters argued, the state of which he is head (Vatican City) is a tiny and insignificant territory – the result of a sordid pact with the fascist dictator Mussolini in 1929?

At the same time as critics sought to downplay the Vatican's status as a state, they also exaggerated it, accusing the Vatican of throwing its diplomatic weight around internationally, lobbying at the United Nations, and frustrating 'progressive' policies around the world by teaming up with Muslims, for example, against 'women's rights'.

Domestically, the Church is accused of interfering in the democratic process in a number of ways: by 'telling Catholics how to vote' at elections; by lobbying governments, bringing to bear its corporate influence on Parliament; and by coercing Catholic politicians into voting according to the Church's diktats under threat of excommunication.

Positive intention

The positive value behind criticism of the Church as a 'self-interested' lobby is that it should be promoting and be driven by the common good, rather than narrow self-interest. The criticism correctly assumes that the Church is founded on another kind of power – covenant relationships, the fruit of communion – and that those who proclaim God should not need to make use of 'the means of this world' to promote God,

> *because Truth persuades on its own merits. Behind the criticism, therefore, is an implicitly Christian view of the Church itself – even if it is a little unreal. True, the Church is not like a corporation. But nor is it disembodied, floating above the world; it is an institution thoroughly in the world, seeking to shape it while looking to a transcendent horizon. Another positive value in the criticism is that the Church should stand for progress in human history, not seek to block it.*

Temporal v spiritual

The neuralgic issue here is the perennial one of 'mixing religion and politics'. Keep in mind the positive intention behind the criticism. Not for nothing did the Second Vatican Council renounce the Church seeking special privileges from the state; the document *Dignitatis Humanae* was a bitter pill for some in countries where the Church had long confused 'Catholic society' with 'Catholic state'. But these were atypical; Christianity is essentially anti-theocratic. The examples of the Church being too close to the state, when faith has been subordinated to party politics, when witness has been diminished and corrupted, are lessons from which the modern Church has learned.

What the secularist critique often forgets is that the radical exclusion of faith from politics has not led to utopia but disaster: the greatest horrors of the twentieth century were inflicted by totalitarian states among whose first moves was the abolition of faith from the public sphere and subordination of religion to the state. Conversely, some of the proudest moments of western political history – the abolition of the slave trade, or the civil rights movement of the 1950s and1960s – are uplifting examples of what happens when churches hold up a transcendent moral horizon to society, and guide the movement that shapes society towards that ideal, seeking to influence the state for the common good. The greatest achievements of western society, in other words, stem from a civilisation in which Church and state coexist and cooperate; the greatest disasters have arisen from efforts by the state to eradicate the Church, often justified by an ideology which interprets the 'will of the people' as a licence for unchecked, unlimited state power.

Christianity believes in keeping the two spheres of faith and politics apart, yet interconnected. Unlike secularism, which proclaims the moral autonomy of the state, a healthy or positive secularity advocates a distinction between faith and politics (but not their divorce). The precise relationship of faith and politics, spiritual and temporal – 'the perennial question of the relationship between what is owed to Caesar and what is owed to God', as Pope Benedict XVI put it when addressing parliamentarians on his UK visit – is a complex one, and there are many different models: the French, the Americans, the British and the Italians, for example, all have contrasting ways of keeping Church and state distinct. But the underlying principle should be clear. Reason and religion need each other. They are intertwined. But they are distinct realms, and should not be confused, both for the sake of the Church and of the state.

Those who resent the Church 'interfering' in politics often object to the perceived politics behind the 'interference', rather than the interference itself. Thus the Church is criticised by the liberal Left in Europe as reactionary or right-wing for opposing 'women's rights' (in arguing against liberal abortion laws) or for being against 'gay rights' (when it opposes, say, same-sex adoption). But the Church is also regularly criticised by the Right for being left-wing in economic and social matters. In Italy, for example, xenophobic immigration policies have been deplored by Catholic leaders – including Vatican officials, leading the Government to describe its church critics as 'Catholic communists' (*cattocommunisti*). Even as gypsies are being rounded up and expelled from Italy and France, they are being very publicly welcomed in the Vatican.

The accusation against the Church for being either right- or left-wing tells you more, therefore, about contemporary politics than about the political inclination of the Church. It will seem both 'right-wing' (in promoting the traditional family, opposing abortion, euthanasia, embryonic research, etc.) *and* 'left-wing' (in advocating the rights of minorities, social justice, active state support for the poorest, etc.), depending on the political bias of the one accusing. The same bias afflicts Catholics. There are pro-life Catholics who think Catholic social teaching is 'socialist', and pro-social justice Catholics who think pro-life causes are right-wing.

The Church will always be accused of 'interfering' or trying to 'impose' its view when the critic disagrees with its stance; but the same critic will say nothing when the Church has intervened politically on a matter he or she agrees with. And if the Church has stayed silent, the critic will accuse it of 'failing to speak out'. Put another way, people are against the Church 'interfering' in what they would much rather be left alone; and in favour of it 'interfering' in what they believe should be changed.

The Church's right to speak out

Why and when does the Church speak out on political questions? The answer is rarely and cautiously, and almost always because it is a matter which touches on the Gospel, on core freedoms and rights (such as the right to life, or to religious freedom), or on core principles of Catholic social teaching. In these cases, the Church not only needs to speak out; it has a *duty* to do so.

The Church promotes active citizenship and political engagement. Christians have always understood themselves to be dual citizens – simultaneously members of the Church and of political society – who must obey the law and work for the good of the Kingdom wherever they are, whatever regime they are under. This 'dual citizenship' is not a divided loyalty; Catholics are both British patriots and loyal to Rome. But living in the world, while looking to a transcendent horizon, produces a tension which is extremely healthy for a democracy, and is one reason why Catholics are unusually active in politics.

Within certain limits (racist parties, for example, are off limits), Catholics are free to vote for whomever they wish; as a body, the Church avoids partisanship – favouring one political party over another – while reserving the right to speak out when a core value is at stake, and encouraging Catholics to enter the political process.

In a modern democracy the Church claims its right to speak out for the same reason that any other civil-society association or organisation does – a natural right to proclaim and promote its values, and to persuade others, to get a debate going about the health of society and its priorities, applying the wisdom and insights of the Christian tradition to the great questions besetting contemporary society. The Church does this because it cares, above all, for the 'common good', meaning that which belongs to all by virtue of their shared humanity. The common good, says the *Catechism of the Catholic Church* (#1906), is 'the sum total of social conditions which allow people, either as groups or as individuals, to reach their fulfilment more fully and more easily'. The common good is a key tenet of the Church's vision for society and the principles which it believes lie behind its healthy functioning.

The argument that the Church 'no longer speaks for the majority' because 'Britain is no longer a Christian society' is true, as far as it goes (which is not very far: considerably more than half of the UK population continues to self-identify as Christian). But the Church's right to speak out has never been dependent on the numbers of its followers. Nor, when it advocates or criticises, is the Church trying to 'impose' its view – although, like others with strong views in a democratic society, it seeks to persuade others. On the other hand, the Church can claim to represent substantial numbers of British citizens, as well as being the world's, and the UK's, largest practising Christian body, and the most significant civil society actor on the world stage. It speaks, what is more, out of a tradition which shaped the moral and cultural values of the western world. And because it is politically and nationally independent, it can ask questions of society that others are not prepared to ask, and speak for those deprived of a voice.

The Church as an international actor

With more than 1.2 billion adherents – about one-fifth of the world's population – the Church is the world's oldest and largest organisation, present through more than 400,000 priests, 800,000 religious sisters and 219,655 parishes. It is the world's second largest international development body (after the UN), and the second largest humanitarian agency (after the Red Cross). Caritas Internationalis, the 60-year-old Rome-based confederation of 165 national bodies of Catholic charities in more than 200 countries, estimates their combined budget at over $5 billion. In Africa the Church runs a quarter of all the hospitals and provides around 12 million school places each year. Globally, it runs more than 5,000 hospitals, 17,500 dispensaries, and 15,000 homes for the elderly, along with tens of thousands of schools. As well as laying claim to be the world's leading moral teacher and guide – an 'expert in humanity', as the Vatican's Justice and Peace Council puts it – the Catholic Church is the largest and most influential actor in global civil society.

Like other global players, it has 'international policy objectives'. The Catholic Church is the only religious body to have an unofficial presence – that of Observer Status – at the United Nations (UN). It is the only religion with a diplomatic corps. But then, the Church is a uniquely significant institution.

Worldwide, the Church is a crucial backer of the Millennium Development Goals (MDGs) and tireless promoter of debt cancellation and other forms of financial aid to the developing world. The Vatican is the world's first carbon-neutral state. The Holy See plays a crucial role in disarmament negotiations and arms trade treaties; in campaigning against the death penalty worldwide; in negotiating the release of hostages; and in conflict resolution. These are the kinds of initiatives which Vatican diplomats are engaged in every day – but which are seldom reported.

These might all be considered 'progressive' initiatives. But the Church would also regard as progressive its opposition to embryonic stem-cell research, liberal abortion laws, and gay adoption; it would see as progressive its opposition to euthanasia and assisted dying, its opposition to the death penalty and its advocacy – in both the UK and the US – of a pathway to citizenship for 'illegal' immigrants who have put down roots in another country. All these are in defence of the dignity of the human person – even if that dignity is not recognised by wider society, because the persons concerned (the unborn, children, the elderly, prisoners, foreign-born) are not seen as 'human beings like us'; or when the rights of particular groups (the victims of crime, a woman with an unplanned pregnancy, a same-sex couple) are seen as in some way absolute or nullifying of the rights of others.

Vatican or Holy See?

Vatican City is a small (if magnificent) area in Rome recognised as a state as a result of the 1929 Lateran

Pacts. The agreement signed with the Italian dictator Benito Mussolini brought to an end a long-running question over the Vatican's territorial sovereignty following the loss of the Papal States and Italy's birth as a nation-state. It is sometimes claimed that the Vatican is only recognised internationally as a state because of that 'sordid pact with a dictator'. But this is to confuse two different things: the Vatican's status as a state, and the international sovereign jurisdiction of the Holy See, which has been recognised for centuries, long before the creation of the Vatican City State.

The diplomatic ties which the UK and other states maintain with the Catholic Church worldwide were not and are not contingent in any way upon that Lateran Pact. Britain's oldest diplomatic relationship, in fact, is with the Holy See – first established formally in 1479, and re-established in 1914, many years before the Pact.

The Holy See is the seat of governance of the worldwide Catholic Church. It has international sovereign jurisdiction, meaning that it is recognised as a legal entity, with which governments have relations. This sovereignty is what enables, for example, the bishop of a local diocese to be appointed by the Vatican, rather than by the local government. This gives the Church an important degree of independence from political power; autocratic governments such as China refuse to accept Rome's right to appoint bishops, regarding it as interference in its sovereign affairs. Religious freedom – the freedom to worship, manifest belief and so on – is safeguarded by the Catholic Church's independence, manifest in its international sovereignty.

Much of what the Holy See achieves worldwide – the result of bringing its moral authority and global presence to bear on countries to help effect change – is possible because of this sovereign international jurisdiction. It means that countries can have formal diplomatic ties with it – just under 200 states do – which in turn means that the Catholic Church can exert its moral influence to make the world a better place. The Holy See has had a continuous history as an organisation since the fourth century, which makes it older than most nation-states. Nor is that relationship one restricted to Catholic countries. Among the many things Britain's diplomats find useful about their links to the Vatican are the Holy See's relationships of trust with nations (Iran, for example) with which the UK has broken political ties. The Vatican's international diplomatic network – the fruit of patient, behind-the-scenes trust-building across the globe – is a vital resource for world peace and cooperation.

The Church's presence in the UK

When the Church raises its voice in UK domestic affairs, it does so by virtue of its moral authority, its independent sovereign jurisdiction, and its strong presence in British civil society. The 6.5 million Catholics in England, Wales, Scotland and Northern Ireland (England and Wales: 5.18 million; Scotland: 695,000; Northern Ireland: 680,000) represent between 10 and 15 per cent of the population. Nor is this affiliation nominal or passive; according to a 2009 MORI poll conducted for the Catholic development agency CAFOD, about 38 per cent of the Catholic population – 2.5 million – goes to Mass at least once a month, demonstrating, by the standards of contemporary society, a highly unusual level of engagement and commitment.

They demonstrate commitment in countless other ways. Practising Catholics play a disproportionately large role in voluntary organisations, welfare agencies and education, and are more likely than the general population to volunteer in every age group. The Church runs 2,300 schools, and 3,000 parishes; there are 4,400 active diocesan priests and more than 5,000 female religious; but the 'Church' is also those hundreds of thousands of Catholics who give their time, energy and money to a huge number of associations of every kind working for the common good.

The Catholic charitable sector in the UK is a massive contributor to the common good of the nation, conspicuous at the sharp edge of society, caring for those whom society has either left behind or scorns: the elderly, the disabled, children, young offenders, the homeless; migrants without papers, travellers and gypsies, seafarers; AIDS sufferers, prisoners, alcoholics, drug addicts, prostitutes ... The list is almost endless.

Catholics reach out to the poorest and most vulnerable irrespective of their beliefs: as many say, 'We care for the poor not because they are Catholics but because we are.' Catholic charitable action is strictly not proselytising: as Pope Benedict XVI says in *Deus Caritas Est* (31c), 'Those who practise charity in the Church's name will never seek to impose the Church's faith upon others.' At the same time, there is no greater witness to Christ's love than to serve the poor both through practical, direct assistance and through advocacy on their behalf, often at the cost of upsetting and challenging existing assumptions and values. In theological terms, Catholic charitable service involves both *diakonia* (showing Christ's love) and *martyrium* (witness).

The national umbrella for Catholic charities in England and Wales, Caritas Social Action Network (CSAN), has begun to map the scale and diversity of Catholic charities. An initial survey in its February 2011 report, *Common Endeavour,* showed that in England and Wales Catholic charities channel the energies of 9,000 employees and 19,000 volunteers in the service of approximately 800,000 people, spending £170 million a year. But it's not just the scale of the Catholic charitable contribution that matters, but the unique way it serves the common good of society.

Catholic charities often do what no one else does, blazing a trail where others later follow – 'out on the edge with those on the edge'; there are countless examples of charitable outreach pioneered by Catholics which over time become 'mainstream' charitable activities; hospices caring for the terminally ill are a prime example. Others remain preserves of the Church. No organisation compares with the Apostleship of the Sea, which provides support and assistance to 200,000 seafarers visiting British ports each year.

Although ultimately inspired by the Gospel – not least the parable of the Good Samaritan and Matthew 25 – most of these charities are directly motivated by the example of a charismatic founder, often a saint. They grow directly out of civil society (rather than as a creation of the state), and frequently depend on and work through parishes and schools, galvanising the energies and passions of networks of volunteers. (Members of the St Vincent de Paul Society of England and Wales, for example, spend 1 million hours each year attending to the socially excluded.) Even though some charities, especially the larger ones, also take public money, they do so far less, on the whole, than other charities: nine out of ten of them receive less than 40 per cent of their support from the state. Finally, they are guided by a coherent set of principles, embodied in Catholic Social Teaching, which in turn enrich British social and political thinking and strengthen civil society. Through CSAN and other nationwide organisations, Catholic charities advocate on behalf of those they serve, influencing policy decisions and helping to shape laws which serve the interests of the poor.

British Catholics also make a massive contribution to overseas development and humanitarian relief through the bishops' agency CAFOD. Founded in 1962, it now has an annual budget of close to £60 million, working with 600 active partners worldwide – usually the local Church – to tackle international poverty. Through its global membership of Caritas Internationalis among other bodies, it has access to decision-makers in Brussels, the United Nations, and other international organisations. CAFOD is one of the five major NGOs (the others are Oxfam, Christian Aid, Save the Children, and ActionAid) which make up the British Overseas Aid Group, or BOAG, which meets government ministers four times a year. Together, CAFOD and CSAN are formidable advocates on behalf of the disadvantaged of British society.

There are 86 Catholic MPs (out of a total of 650), sitting in Parliament, plus five Sinn Fein MPs who have not taken their seats. Of the sitting MPs, close to two-thirds (51) are Labour, 26 are Conservative, five Lib-Dem, three SNP and one SDLP. The predominance of Labour reflects the historical identification of working-class Irish immigrants with the party (most British Catholics are originally from Labour districts) although Catholics no longer vote Labour *en bloc*.

The Catholic Bishops' Conference employs a full-time public policy officer to develop links between Parliament and the Church. The conference secretariat is frequently invited to comment on forthcoming legislation. Lines of communication are kept open between 10 Downing Street and the Archbishop of Westminster.

There is nothing odd or sinister about this. Many large organisations which lay claim to a significant influence over sectors of public opinion – trade unions, faiths, business associations, and so on – are regularly con-sulted by Government, make representations to Govern-ment, and can expect to be listened to when laws are being formulated that could affect the lives of the people these organisations represent. It would be a very poor and authoritarian government which regarded its electoral majority as a mandate to govern without consultation.

Bishops and elections

Every five years, when a general election is called, the Catholic bishops of England and Wales issue a document well in advance of the polling date which sets out some of the considerations they believe voters should keep in mind when they cast their vote. They are *not* advocating one particular party or another; their aim is instead to influence all parties and their platforms – and to mobilise the electorate to take a clear interest in their local candidates. In politics, it is normal to seek to persuade others of your vision; everyone in politics is, in that sense, trying to 'impose' their values by the force of persuasion.

In 2010, the bishops took the unusual step of also issuing a general document in response to the global political and economic crisis. 'Choosing the Common Good', a reflection on the British crisis in the light of Pope Benedict XVI's encyclical *Caritas in Veritate*, called for a restoration of trust in British institutions. Later, the bishops' standard 'considerations for voters' document drew out some of the themes in that previous one: valuing life; family; migration; development of the world's poor; environment; and the importance of religious belief in the public square.

The questions which the bishops posed were ones which they intended voters to put to their constituency candidates, questions such as: 'What does respect for life mean for you?', 'Do all lives have the same value?', 'What will you do for marriage and the family?', 'What beliefs and values underpin your approach to migration?' and 'What do you think is the place of religion in society?' The list, the bishops stressed, 'was not exhaustive' but was intended to help voters form an idea of how far a candidate will address the common good.

Underneath the questions were five 'statements of value':

1. Valuing life … means opposing abortion and euthanasia, and life-cramping poverty, and neglect of the elderly.
2. Families are the basic building-block of any stable society. Marriage provides the best context for bringing up children and must have the clear support and encouragement of Government.
3. Migration is not about numbers, it is about human beings. Wherever the Government sets the boundary on who can or cannot live here, it must apply its rules with fairness, decency and respect for the individual.
4. Our care for each other is also shown in how we support the development of the world's poorest people, and how we use – or abuse – the environment we share. We must be good stewards of God's creation, not selfish exploiters of it.
5. Our faith is at the heart of our lives. Religious belief is not something private: it helps create a society that wants to see everyone flourish. It has a contribution to make and must be allowed to do so in accordance with its teachings.

With this list, bishops were not telling Catholics which party to vote for; they were asking them to inject into the electoral process values which were at risk of being forgotten, to raise the standards of election debates beyond the competitiveness and pragmatism of electoral politics.

Because the Catholic Church is a large, organised body, which every day demonstrates its commitment to building up British society, it has some political weight; it is listened to and can make its voice heard on the issues of the day. But that doesn't mean its influence is disproportionate or excessive. As we will see with the adoption agencies row [see Chapter 3], the Church frequently loses – even where its basic rights and freedoms are concerned.

Still, say critics, even if the bishops claim not to be urging Catholics to vote for one party or another, they are in practice doing so, because comparing the bishops' list to the party platforms can usually lead to only one conclusion. Yet if that were true, Catholics would vote the same way at elections; in fact, the Catholic vote is scattered across the three parties. More Catholics voted for Labour in 1997 than voted Conservative; but in 2010 the reverse was true. Voting in a general election should be about deciding which government would best be likely to promote the common good, and there are a range of interests and concerns which go into making up that decision.

Church, conscience and politicians

Another objection to the Church's involvement in the political sphere is that it threatens Catholic politicians with excommunication if they fail to 'toe the line' on questions such as abortion. In this way, say critics, the Church interferes in the democratic process, seeking to 'impose its view' through the use of a kind of moral coercion.

But there is another consideration. The Church also has to maintain its internal good order, and one of the obligations of bishops is to act to make clear when church teaching on vital questions is being misrepresented by people in public positions in such a way as risks misleading the faithful.

The issue has arisen specifically in the case of abortion and euthanasia, because these are concerned with the sanctity of life, which the Church believes should be reflected in society's rule of law, defending 'the basic right to life from conception to natural death'. This right holds a 'unique place' in Catholic Social Teaching, notes the prefect of the Congregation for the Doctrine of the Faith, Cardinal Levada, so that 'there may be legitimate diversity of opinion even among Catholics about waging war and applying the death penalty, but not with regard to abortion and euthanasia'. In order for a Catholic to be in full communion with the faith of the Church, therefore, he or she must accept this teaching; referring to laws which promote or authorise abortion and euthanasia, Pope John Paul II's encyclical letter *Evangelium Vitae* says, there is 'a grave and clear obligation to oppose them by conscientious objection' (no. 73).

What should the Church do about politicians who advertise themselves as Catholics but who vote time and again to liberalise abortion laws, or to undermine attempts at restricting those laws? In January 2004, when the Democrat candidate John Kerry was campaigning in the diocese of St Louis, its then Archbishop, now Cardinal, Raymond Burke announced he would refuse the candidate Communion. Kerry was a Mass-goer, and wanted to take advantage of the kudos which in the US attaches to churchgoing politicians by advertising himself as a Catholic; but he also had a notoriously pro-abortion voting record, and Archbishop Burke wanted to make clear that these two things were incompatible. Burke's stance was supported by some other US bishops. But it was resisted by others, including Kerry's own bishop, Cardinal Séan O'Malley of Boston, who were anxious not to politicise the Eucharist.

In the end the bishops met in June 2004 and agreed to disagree. 'Given the wide range of circumstances involved in arriving at a prudential judgement' on the question, their statement read, 'bishops can legitimately make different judgements on the most prudent course of pastoral action. Such decisions, the statement concluded, 'rest with the individual bishop in accord with established canonical and pastoral principles.'

Their statement, 'Catholics in political life', was issued after reading a memorandum by the then Cardinal prefect of the Congregation for the Doctrine of the Faith, Joseph Ratzinger. In it he advised US bishops to speak *privately* with prominent Catholics who defy church teachings on key issues involving the sanctity of life, alert them to the gravity of their offences, and warn them that they will be refused Communion if they do not change their ways. Only if these warnings are not heeded, Cardinal Ratzinger added, 'and the person in question, with obstinate persistence, still presents himself to receive the Holy Eucharist, the minister of Holy Communion must refuse to distribute it.'

The issue for the bishops, in other words, was not how to influence the outcome of an election or a politician's voting record, but how to deal with a particular scandal arising from a public Catholic who was publicly violating Church teaching in an essential matter of ethics. It was precisely because Archbishop Burke's stance risked influencing how Catholics might vote that some other bishops were reluctant to follow his example. Cardinal Ratzinger's solution reflected this concern; he advocated the public disbarring from Communion only as a matter of last resort. The Church upholds as an important first principle that political battles should be fought, in the words of the Archbishop of Washington at the time, Cardinal Theodore McCarrick, 'not at the Communion rail but in the public square, in hearts and minds, in our pulpits and public advocacy, in our consciences and communities'.

What the Church stands for

It is up to Catholics involved in politics to make up their own minds about which parties to support, and why. Their priorities and concerns will differ; so will their loyalties and their affiliations. But there are key principles on which all Catholics should agree, because they have been consistently taught by the Church since 1891, when Pope Leo XIII issued the first 'social encyclical' of modern times, *Rerum Novarum*. Since then, there have been many more encyclicals, and many other church documents, expanding on and applying these principles to contemporary challenges. Catholic social teaching (CST) offers a set of principles for reflection, criteria for judgement and directives for action. Its purpose is to contribute to the formation of conscience as a basis for specific action. It amounts, in effect, to a Catholic vision of politics, society and the economy.

CST, which came into being in response to the development of modern western capitalism, has two major concerns. The first is the alienation between capital and labour – the division of society into those who control wealth and property, and the majority who have to sell their labour. (It was the growth of the poverty-stricken masses in the cities of Europe which sparked Pope Leo's encyclical.) The second is the growth in the power of the market and the state, and the reduction in the size and the strength of civil society – sometimes known as the 'third sector'.

Put positively, the popes in 17 key social encyclicals since 1891 have urged two essential reforms to the modern liberal market polity and economy. The first is the 'humanisation' of the market, putting people before profits, and remembering the human purpose of the economy. The second is a call for a strengthened civil society, made up of vigorous 'intermediate associations', as opposed to a society seen as made up only of the state, capital and isolated individuals.

CST has a number of key principles set out in a series of papal encyclicals and other church documents over time: dignity of the human person, the common good, just wage, the universal destination of goods, solidarity, subsidiarity, participation, option for the poor, peace and disarmament, the preservation of life and creation, and the call to action. Each of these themes is a rich mine of insight and wisdom into the right ordering of a modern, democratic, pluralist society.

The Catholic political agenda is also marked by its strong advocacy of religious freedom, considered by the Church to be the first and most fundamental of all basic rights, from which all others flow. The enemies of religious freedom are both fundamentalism and secularism.

'The same determination that condemns every form of fanaticism and religious fundamentalism must also oppose every form of hostility to religion that would restrict the public role of believers in civil and political life,' said Pope Benedict in his 1 January 2011 message. 'Religious fundamentalism and secularism are alike in that both represent extreme forms of a rejection of legitimate pluralism and the principle of secularity.'

Religious freedom is not just immunity from coercion in matters of conscience – the freedom to reject faith and God, or to convert from one faith to another. It is also, says Pope Benedict, 'the ability to order one's own choices in accordance with truth'. The recognition of this freedom is the bedrock of pluralism and democracy, because it implies that God and conscience precede the state; the state, with its coercive power, is not the arbiter of consciences, conceding rights, but at the service of a society made up of many different ideas about truth. What undermines religious freedom, therefore, is what distorts the delicate balance between temporal and spiritual, leading to the eclipse of one by the other, which in turn produces (eventually) fundamentalism enthroned in theocracy, or relativism enthroned in totalitarianism. As Pope Benedict said in his address at Westminster Hall in September 2010: 'the world of reason and the world of faith – the world of secular rationality and the world of religious belief – need one another and should not be afraid to enter into profound and on-going dialogue, for the good of our civilization.'

What makes the Church's thinking on politics distinctive? Here are nine suggestions:

1. The inherent God-endowed dignity of every human being, however feeble or sinful, must be respected; that is the starting-point for a moral vision of society.

2. Men and women are social beings whose rights and responsibilities are realised in community and relationship; politics is not just about competing individual rights, but primarily about seeking the common good, understood as those social conditions which enable people to flourish.

3. Solidarity: the moral test of a society lies in how it treats its vulnerable members; special attention must be given to those less able to participate in society, whether through material poverty, disability, immigration status, old age, illness, addiction, imprisonment etc.

4. Subsidiarity: a society is best governed in such a way that the decisions are taken at the closest possible level to those affected by them; this principle means that it is wrong for the state to take over that which is better managed locally or lower down. But it also means that the state cannot abrogate its responsibility to act when it is appropriate to do so.

5. Societies should aim at increasing levels of participation in decision-making, especially by those excluded from the body politic.

6. The Church is pro-life, and calls for the laws of the land to protect life; it opposes, therefore, laws allowing abortion, euthanasia, capital punishment, embryonic stem-cell research and other practices which deliberately terminate God-given human life.

7. The Church favours a 'humanised' or 'civil' market as the most efficient means of achieving sustainable prosperity, but rejects Darwinian conceptions of the

market. Employers may succeed, for example, in persuading workers to accept levels of pay that are insufficient for the core needs of a person and their family; but that does not make it a just contract. The Church argues in favour of a 'just' wage – otherwise known as a 'family' or 'living wage' – as the necessary minimum, whatever the market may determine, in the same way that it opposes 'usury' – the charging of excessive interest, whether or not the lending is legal.

8. The Church calls for a society and an economy in which trust and virtue, rather than purely utilitarian concerns, are paramount; and in which the depersonalising impact of technology and bureaucracy can be countered by a vigorous civil society in which bonds of gift and reciprocity matter more than contracts.

9. The Church calls for the well-off to 'live simply' in order to lessen the burden on the planet and help poorer nations to develop.

From these broad principles many possible policies flow: progressive taxation, labour protection, free schools, living-wage mandates, carbon tax, paternity leave, regularisation of long-term undocumented migrants, foreign debt remissions, and so on. But while bishops have often advocated such policies, it is usually a matter for politicians to devise the specific policies which help advance the general principles.

Existing frame
'The Catholic Church uses its power and influence to advance a reactionary agenda designed to frustrate

progress in human rights and liberties. Bishops tell people how to vote, and threaten politicians with excommunication when they don't do the Pope's bidding. The Church is essentially right-wing, seeking to impose outdated views on a secular state and on people who have no Christian allegiance.'

Reframe

The Church raises its voice in the public sphere whenever an issue touches on the common good, especially on questions of basic freedoms and rights, and especially when it can be a voice for the voiceless. Its authority to speak out derives from its moral authority and independence as one of the world's leading and oldest civil society organisations. It is neither right- nor left-wing, and has no allegiance to particular political parties, but exists to defend the common good and the Gospel in its integrity. It defends, and speaks up for, a distinction between the political and the religious; it upholds what it calls a 'positive secularity', and deplores both religious fundamentalism and an aggressive kind of secularism which seek to banish faith from the public square. When it deplores politicians who claim to be Catholic while advocating, for example, abortion and euthanasia, it is not trying to coerce politicians but to prevent scandal. The Catholic Church's political agenda can be summed up as Catholic social teaching plus religious freedom, the freedom which underlies all other rights and freedoms.

Key messages

- The Church has a natural right to speak out, derived from its moral authority and its presence in society.
- The Church advocates religious freedom and the proper distinction between faith and politics. It calls for the political and the religious to be in dialogue, not separated.
- Bishops do not speak out before elections to persuade Catholics to vote one way or another; they identify the issues which Catholics should be concerned about, and addressing their politicians on.
- The Catholic Church's political agenda can be summed up in Catholic social teaching and religious freedom. It is neither left nor right wing but an agenda which is the bedrock of freedom and civilisation.

Chapter 2

Homosexuality and contraception

Challenging questions

- *Why is the Church in favour of family planning but not contraception?*
- *If Catholics in this country ignore the Church's teaching and use contraception, why should anyone listen to what the Church says?*
- *If God created people as gay why wouldn't he want them to have committed sexual relationships?*
- *If the Church regards gay people as 'disordered', how can it oppose discrimination against them?*

Few issues are as neuralgic as homosexuality and contraception, which belong here together because they concern the purpose and morality of sex. The idea that sex might have a purpose or meaning – a 'good' – is nowadays countercultural: the common view is that if sex is consensual, it is legitimate. Yet most people in their hearts know that sex is or should be more than pleasure-seeking between consenting adults, and should involve some degree of affection or commitment – or at least avoid commodification: extra-marital affairs, for example, are broadly disapproved of even though they are consensual. Most people agree, then, that sex needs to have the right *context* in order to fulfil its purposes, which in turn presupposes boundaries – although many would disagree where those boundaries lie. In short, it is not just the Church which believes in sexual morality – even if sometimes it seems that only the Church is prepared publicly to say what that morality should look like.

There is widespread confusion about what moral constraints on sex should exist. Some look to the law, which draws boundaries, mostly based on the principle of consent; but many of these are necessarily arbitrary, especially when it comes to the age at which the law regards people as being capable of consenting. (An adult who has sex with a teenager whose sixteenth birthday falls on 30 June commits an illegal act the day before, and a perfectly legal one the day after. This tells us nothing about the morality of the act.)

The Church, in contrast, offers a bold and clear view of sex, one in keeping with the wisdom and insight of the ages – but not locked into the past. Drawing on the wisdom and insight not just of Revelation but of centuries of reflection on the experience of human relationships, it holds that sex is essentially 'good' if it occurs within a marriage between a man and a woman and is open to children; in this case, it conforms to God's design and is both procreative and unitive – that is, it deepens the bond between the man and the woman because it is open to new life. Outside that context, on the other hand, sex can be egotistical, destructive and the cause of profound alienation between human beings.

Much has been written in church documents since the Second Vatican Council, and especially in the teaching of Pope John Paul II known as Theology of the Body, about the power, beauty and meaning of conjugal love. It is no longer true to say that either society or the Church regards the sole purpose of marriage to be children; its other essential purpose is 'the good of the spouses', or conjugal love. There is nothing old-fashioned, therefore, about the Catholic view of marriage: modern theology regards it as a vehicle for happiness and fulfilment. But there is also a radical, counter-cultural element of the Catholic view of marriage, which is that the two elements – the love of the spouses, and openness to children – are intertwined and should not be separated.

There are, therefore, two neuralgic elements in the question of sex and the Church. The first is the Church's teaching that sex belongs within marriage. The second is the Church's teaching that, within marriage, sex must be open to procreation. Both of these can be – and usually are – expressed negatively: the Church is against sex outside marriage, including homosexuality; and the Church is opposed to contraception, which severs the link between sex and children. Expressed positively, however, this teaching is an inspiring and uplifting one, and the reframing of this issue should reflect the beauty of the Church's insights.

The meaning of sex

Sex has a meaning, direction and purpose. It can take us further away from, or further towards, the good for which it is intended. The degree of consent underpinning most modern views of sex ('as long as no one gets hurt') is insufficient: just because it is consented, doesn't make it good, however much it may be sought or desired or freely engaged in, if it occurs outside the security and commitment of lifelong trust and intimacy between a husband and wife.

For proof that this is so, there is no shortage of evidence around us in the everyday experience of hurt and rejection. Who has not known, or does not know another who has known, the searing feeling of being treated as an object of desire, rather than an object of love? The deepest love must involve self-giving, surrender, a change in the way people focus their attention and energies onto another, and the security of a lifelong commitment; when sex happens without this change, a person is 'lying' with their body – they undermine something essential to the meaning of love. Sex can become simply an appetite with a tendency to treat persons as objects, which is why, perhaps, the modern experience of promiscuity is one of gratification followed quickly by boredom (people quickly tire of objects) and the feeling – by at least of one of the parties – of being 'used'. Because this feeling is so common – almost universal – among those who have sex outside marriage, it suggests that sex does have a meaning or design or intrinsic purpose, a meaning which involves commitment, trust and self-giving. The feeling of being 'used' is usually accompanied by a horrible sense that we have given away too much of ourselves. One of the things we surrender in the act of love is knowledge about ourselves that we should only give away to someone to whom we have pledged – and has pledged to us – lifelong love.

Catholic Voices can begin this discussion therefore not needing to feel defensive; judging by the misery in contemporary society, it is the modern permissive view of sexuality, rather than the Catholic view, which requires a systematic defence. This is above all true when we consider the impact on children, who are the product of sex, whether intended or unintended, planned or unplanned. Children require, above all, stability for their healthy development – which is the one thing that unmarried couples cannot offer them. Fewer than one in ten cohabiting relationships lasts more than ten years.

That said, there is no doubt that the Church presents to our age a demanding understanding and ethic of marriage and sexuality, one that is often difficult to realise in practice and which even practising Catholics either ignore or fall from; and this is particularly true in the case of contraception, where magisterial teaching is at least as often ignored as it is followed.

To criticise it can seem that, if church teaching is not accepted by Catholics, it is hardly likely to have any relevance to wider society. But this does not follow. Many church teachings over the centuries have failed, in one generation or another, to convince the majority of the faithful. The Church has always taught the universal destination of material goods and the need to make responsible use of possessions (to 'live simply', as CAFOD puts it). Yet often Catholics have amassed large wealth with little or no concern for their neighbour. Or, to take another example, substantial numbers of American Catholics continue to advocate the death penalty for crimes such as murder, despite the clear opposition of the *Catechism* and the US bishops.

Jesus' own followers frequently threw up their hands in despair at the apparent impossibility of obeying his teaching; the Church, Christ's instrument on earth, is frequently resented for making unrealistic demands on its followers. Yet attitudes change; the Church develops; the faithful learn; what one age regards as impossible and unrealistic another will see as normal and right, and vice versa. Sometimes the Church can be 'out of touch' with the modern age because it is radically ahead of it – even of its own followers.

Positive intention

The positive intention behind the criticism of the Church's teaching on homosexuality and contraception is tied to concern for people's welfare and dignity, and an awareness of the wrongness of scapegoating and condemnation. Contraception is seen as protecting people from the consequences of their actions – unplanned pregnancy – which could affect the lives of many.

The positive intention behind the criticism therefore expresses concern at the possibility of people being harmed or sacrificed for the sake of dogmas and principles, and compassion for people who are not ready or willing to embrace conjugal love. Recognising this concern and compassion as being essentially Christian, a Catholic Voice needs to appeal to that same concern and compassion in explaining the Church's view.

Contraception

Church teaching is adamant that the deliberate decision to separate sex and fertility undermines the purpose and meaning of sex itself. The increasing use of contraception shows that sex and procreation are being pulled ever further apart.

In the 1983 *Code of Canon Law* marriage is described as a partnership (*consortium*) for the whole of life, which is ordered co-equally to two good ends: the good of the spouses (*bonum coniugum*) and the procreation and education of children (*bonum prolis*). The Second Vatican Council made clear that children are not the only purpose of marriage; conjugal love and children are equally important ends– indeed are vitally linked. The key document setting this out, Pope Paul VI's 1968 encyclical, *Humanae Vitae*, refers to the 'unitive' and the 'procreative' elements of sex, and says they should not be separated.

Because the purpose of sex is conjugal love, and because one of the essential 'ends' of marriage is children, contraception – which suppresses the capacity for procreation – is wrong, for it 'closes the sexual act to the gift of life'. Contraception deliberately makes the sexual act infertile, by, for example, suppressing the production of eggs (the Pill) or preventing the transmission of sperm (condoms). Contraception is described in *Humanae Vitae* #14 (restated in the *Catechism* #2370) as an action which, 'whether in anticipation of the conjugal act, or in its accomplishment, or in the development of its natural consequences, proposes [*intendat*], whether as an end or as a means, to render procreation impossible'. Contraception is not, in other words, simply an action which impedes procreation, but an action impeding procreation carried out with an intent to do so. (As *Humanae Vitae* notes, using anti-ovulatory pills for medical reasons such as stemming excessive blood loss is not a form of contraception in the moral sense.)

But being opposed to contraception doesn't make Catholics 'natalist' – in favour of enormous families. A married couple needs to 'regulate' (in the *Catechism*'s words) the number of children they have, and it is 'one of the aspects of responsible fatherhood and motherhood' to do so (#2399.) The question is how to do so in morally acceptable ways – respecting the meaning and purpose of sex rather than attempting to alter it.

Explaining why one is right and the other wrong is at the heart of what needs to be communicated on this point. This is not easy, because the Church's teaching starts from an assumption that is not widely shared – that sex has an intrinsic purpose (marriage that welcomes children); and because, for most people (including many Catholics) regulating births is synonymous with contraception.

Why contraception is wrong but NFP is OK

The Church's opposition to contraception has been constant from the earliest age: it has been seen as frustrating God's creative power, in which human beings are his partner.

This was the teaching of all the Christian Churches until 1930, when the Anglican Church at its Lambeth Conference voted that 'if there was morally sound reasoning for avoiding abstinence' as a means of limiting births, then 'other methods may be used, provided that this is done in the light of Christian principles.' The 1958 Lambeth Conference resolved that the number and frequency of children was laid by God upon the consciences of parents 'in such ways as are acceptable to husband and wife'.

The Catholic Church, however, maintained the traditional Christian position, expressed in *Casti Connubi* (Pius XI, 1931): 'Since, therefore, the conjugal act is destined primarily by nature for the begetting of children, those who in exercising it deliberately frustrate its natural power and purpose sin against nature.' Pius XII upheld this teaching and developed it, allowing for the use of the infertile period to regulate births. At the Second Vatican Council, the role which sex plays in marriage in deepening 'conjugal love' between the husband and wife was stressed, along with the procreative element; this marked an important shift from a previous era in which marriage was seen primarily, or sometimes exclusively, as an institution for the fostering of children and for social stability. The 1968 encyclical *Humanae Vitae* developed the links between the two aspects, unitive and procreative, noting that 'to experience the gift of married love while respecting the laws of conception is to acknowledge that one is not the master of the sources of life but rather the minister of the design established by the Creator' (#13).

In Canon Law, consistent and constant use of contraception may demonstrate that an intention against children is 'firm, intense, inflexible and non-negotiable' on the part of the couple, or one of them; in which case, it invalidates the marriage, because an essential property of marriage, the *bonum prolis*, has been excluded.

Assuming there isn't an intention on the part of the married couple to exclude children altogether, the Church encourages them to discern how many children it is responsible and right for them to have. 'Let them thoughtfully take into account both their own welfare and that of their children, those already born and those which the future may bring,' the Catholic bishops of the world declared in the Second Vatican Council document *Gaudium et Spes* (#50). 'For this accounting they need to reckon with both the material and the spiritual conditions of the times as well as of their state in life. Finally, they should consult the interests of the family group, of temporal society, and of the Church herself.'

The modern method recommended by the Church for spacing children is known as natural family planning (NFP), of which there are a number of models or techniques. The spread and popularity of workshops and courses teaching these methods add up to a largely unreported 'quiet revolution' in contemporary society, similar, in some ways, to the rise in new habits of ecological awareness such as recycling. Sadly, Catholics are almost as likely as everyone else to be ignorant of these techniques, which are at least as effective as contraceptive methods in enabling couples to plan births, yet unlike contraceptive methods, they do not suppress fertility.

Why is using this 'natural' method of preventing conception acceptable, but not 'artificial' methods? There are many good 'organic' reasons: women are increasingly aware of the damaging effects of the Pill and its side effects. Hormonal pills have a dampening effect on sexual libido. Many so-called contraceptives, such as the morning-after pill are in fact abortefacients. And with 'typical use', the failure rate of the Pill can be as high as 8 per cent – because some women forget to take it every day. Modern women are turning against the Pill for many of the same reasons that they are turning against chemical-industrial food production or certain kinds of chemical cosmetics.

But while there is much to be said about how much better (for people, for the planet) are natural methods, it is not because contraception is 'artificial' that the Church rejects it (or it would need to deplore paracetamol), but because contraception denies the purpose of the sexual act, and severs that act from its meaning. What is wrong is not the 'unnaturalness' of the act, but the very attempt to have sex while simultaneously and intentionally trying to deprive it of its procreative purpose. Natural methods work with, and in conformity to, nature's own cycles, cycles which are designed to enable procreation only some of the time.

NFP and artificial contraception are very different: when used by couples to space children, sex using NFP is *non-procreative*, because it takes place during the infertile part of the woman's cycle; but artificial birth control enables sex that is *anti-procreative*. The couple using NFP is accepting their fertility as it is: a great good, but a good which they are not going to use at this time. The husband respects his wife's cycle and does not try to manipulate it or suppress it. Where a couple using artificial birth control treats their fertility as an inconvenience, a defect in need of improvement, or an illness, a couple using NFP recognises fertility as a good and does nothing to deny this good.

They also produce different kinds of behaviour. NFP requires self-mastery, a virtue developed through periodic abstinence; it strengthens the powers and the virtues of the human person, and makes it more likely that the sexual act be the product of a desire to express love for another, not the outcome of an ungovernable passion. As *Humanae Vitae* observes (#21), such self-discipline 'brings to family life abundant fruits of tranquillity and peace. It helps in solving difficulties of other kinds. It fosters in husband and wife thoughtfulness and loving consideration for one another. It helps them to repel inordinate self-love, which is the opposite of charity. It arouses in them a consciousness of their responsibilities. And finally, it confers upon parents a deeper and more effective influence in the education of their children.'

The Church sees the powerful link between the proper use of sexuality, the strength of marriage, and the health of society. Key to all three is sexual self-discipline, which is necessary for deepening conjugal love. Contraception undermines that discipline; NFP builds it.

Homosexuality and the purpose of sex

'Sexuality has an intrinsic meaning and direction, which is not homosexual,' says Pope Benedict XVI in *Light of the World* (*LoW*); for 'evolution has brought forth sexuality for the purpose of reproducing the species'. The idea that sex has an intrinsic purpose and meaning may seem strange to an age which regards it as the expression of intimacy or an act of pleasure. Yet however counter-cultural, what the Church teaches is quite in keeping with history and culture: the purpose and meaning of sex is to unite a man and a woman in order to give children a future. 'This is the determination internal to the essence of sexuality,' Pope Benedict adds. 'Everything else is against sexuality's intrinsic meaning and direction.'

The Pope recognises how unpopular this teaching is: 'this is a point we need to hold firm,' he says, 'even if it is not pleasing to our age.' The issue at stake here, he goes on, 'is the intrinsic truth of sexuality's significance in the constitution of man's being.'

A Catholic Voice on these issues needs, above all, to be able to explain what the Church teaches, and the reasons that support that teaching, as well as to dispel a number of myths which are often angrily thrown at the Church – that it 'calls gay people disordered' or 'is against gay rights'. Because many people's experience of sexuality – and this may be true above all for gay people – is frequently one of hurt, anger and indignation are never far below the surface. It is important to hear the positive intention behind those critiques before showing the depth and beauty of the Church's call to conjugal love.

The Church and homophobia

The Church's teaching is sometimes described by critics as reflecting a visceral (homophobic) prejudice against gay people. Yet the *Catechism* (#2357) has a very accurate and straightforward definition of homosexuality as referring to 'relations between men or between women who experience an exclusive or predominant sexual attraction toward persons of the same sex', and goes on to point out that this is nothing new: homosexuality 'has taken a great variety of forms through the centuries and in different cultures', says the *Catechism*, before adding that 'its psychological genesis remains largely unexplained'. The Church therefore does not take a position on the unresolved 'nature versus nurture' debate about why some people are homosexually inclined; and therefore cannot be accused of homophobic ideas and language about gay people being in some way 'unnatural'.

Nor does the Church reject – as homophobes often do – the prevalence of the homosexual inclination: 'the number of men and women who have deep-seated homosexual tendencies is *not negligible*' (#2358), says the *Catechism* – not something that homophobes would ever accept.

Note this term 'deep-seated' – sometimes translated as 'deeply rooted' – used by the *Catechism*. Sexuality is complicated. People change and develop. There is a common phenomenon of a 'gay phase' in many young people's lives, when awakening sexual feelings can be directed towards people of the same sex, as a kind of precursor to attractions to those of the opposite sex. The Church recognises this, and does not consider it to be homosexuality unless those feelings develop into a 'deep-seated' – that is, a lasting and definite – orientation.

The *Catechism* spends some time opposing homophobia, using very strong language about the importance of accepting gay people with 'respect, compassion and sensitivity', adding firmly that 'every sign of unjust discrimination in their regard should be avoided'.

Indeed nothing in the Church's official teaching on homosexuality justifies the accusation that it is contributing to the marginalisation of, or prejudice against, gay people. In the UK, the Church publicly welcomed the Wolfenden Report, which urged the decriminalisation of private homosexual acts as long ago as 1957. It has continued to welcome many other significant changes in the law that have removed unjust discrimination against people on the grounds of their sexuality. And it has consistently worked to bring down the barriers of prejudice in society and in the workplace which have prevented gay people (and other minorities) from playing their full role in society. It is therefore wrong to claim, as some do, that the Church 'is opposed to gay rights' – even though it is strongly opposed to some laws which have been advanced in the name of gay rights. The Church believes, for example, that marriage is a natural institution between a man and a woman; other kinds of union are not marriage. This is not an anti-gay rights position, but a pro-marriage one.

Much of the modern 'gay rights' agenda, in fact, has little to do with the original purpose of the movement to end prejudice and hostility against homosexual people in the law and in public opinion. In the 1980s, the Archbishop of Westminster, Cardinal Basil Hume, set down criteria for Catholics considering how to respond to proposed changes in the law claiming to eliminate discrimination or prejudice against gay people, but which may conceal other agendas or curb other rights. 'Are there reasonable grounds for judging that the institution of marriage and the family could, and would, be undermined by a change in the law? Would society's rejection of a proposed change in the law be more harmful to the common good than the acceptance of such a change? Does a person's sexual orientation or activity constitute, in specific circumstances, a sufficient and relevant reason for treating that person in any way differently from other citizens?'

Cardinal Hume said these were 'matters of practical judgment and assessment of social consequences, and thus must be considered case by case – and this without prejudice to Catholic teaching concerning homosexual acts.'

Those last words are significant. Catholics are quite able to distinguish between the moral question of homosexuality – sex is reserved for marriage – and the civil rights of gay people. The Church believed both that homosexual acts are immoral and favoured their decriminalisation; in the same way, the Church opposes all 'unjust' discrimination against gay people while at the same time upholding the unique importance of marriage in law. Catholics can applaud and welcome the lifting of obstacles to the participation in civic life of gay people of recent years, while opposing attempts to enthrone an ideology which seeks to establish same-sex unions as equal in law to the marriage of a man and a woman – and what flows from this: same-sex adoption.

Just as the Church's opposition to same-sex marriage derives from its belief that a marriage between a man and a woman is in the best interests of society, so its opposition to same-sex adoption derives from its conviction that a child's best interests are served by being brought up by a man and a woman. It is not that the Church in each case 'opposes gay rights'; it is that the Church is in favour of the rights of children, and the duty of the state to protect marriage.

So when the Church opposes attempts by the state to give special protection and rights to same-sex unions (or indeed to any sexual relations outside marriage) or same-sex adoption, it is not seeking to enforce prejudice against gay people; it is arguing that the good of society and children are best protected by reserving some legal privileges to marriage and restrictions on the right to adopt. There are many different rights at stake in this question: the common good of society, the rights of children, and so on. Legislating for gay 'rights' to marriage and adoption creates new victims. A focus that puts the child first leads naturally to opposing same-sex marriage and adoption.

And here is the neuralgic point between the Church and some gay rights advocates. The legal strategy employed by some gay lobbies has been to secure the passage of sexual orientation anti-discrimination laws, and then invoke the principle embedded within those laws as a basis for same-sex 'marriage' and same-sex adoption. Anti-discrimination legislation in this way has become a mechanism for dethroning marriage as an institution privileged by law, and for enthroning a new principle – that same-sex unions are equivalent to marriage between a man and a woman, and same-sex adoption is equivalent to adoption by a mother and father. Thereafter it is a small step to compel all institutions to accept that principle or face the consequences (as has occurred with the Catholic adoption agencies, see Chapter 3).

Thus, says Pope Benedict in *LoW*, 'in the name of tolerance, tolerance is being abolished'. A new orthodoxy, backed by the state, has driven out the old: 'Christianity finds itself exposed now to an intolerant pressure that at first ridicules it – as belonging to a perverse, false way of thinking – and then tries to deprive it of breathing space in the name of an ostensible rationality' (#53).

Yet the fact that the Church opposes the dethroning of marriage does not mean it necessarily opposes civil rights for cohabiting couples – including same-sex ones. If by 'civil partnerships' is meant enabling cohabiting couples (which would include same-sex couples, sisters, maiden aunts, long-term carers and patients) to have next-of-kin rights (to visit in hospital, inherit etc.), the Church has no difficulty in principle: the law may encourage, for the common good, stable domestic arrangements. In a 2011 statement, the Catholic bishops of England and Wales noted that 'the Church recognised the need to address legal, financial, and property difficulties faced by same-sex couples long before the Civil Partnership Act. However, it believed – and continues to believe – that this could be done without the need for civil partnerships, and in particular without the attempt to set up civil partnership as though it were the same as marriage.' It went on to add that 'the practical benefits of a civil partnership should not be the exclusive property of those in a homosexual relationship.'

In legislating for civil partnerships, the Government in 2003 claimed that they were not marriages. Yet a civil partnership is a civil arrangement available only to non-related people of the same sex who take vows and receive legal privileges identical to those of marriage. Further moves are now afoot to allow civil partnerships to be solemnised in churches and synagogues. While denying that it is doing so, the British state has been redefining marriage.

'Marriage does not belong to the state any more than it belongs to the Church,' said Archbishop Peter Smith in response to the Government's announcement of a consultation in early 2011. Marriage is 'a fundamental human institution rooted in human nature itself', he added, entailing 'a lifelong commitment of a man and a woman to each other, publicly entered into, for their mutual well-being and for the procreation and upbringing of children'. As such, he went on, 'no authority – civil or religious – has the power to modify the fundamental nature of marriage.'

In short, the Church does not oppose extending civil rights and legal privileges to long-term, stable, cohabiting couples, but opposes these being restricted to same-sex couples. The nature of that restriction, and the proposal now to allow those couples to solemnise their partnerships in churches, suggest that the state is currently trying to recast marriage in such a way that it is no longer exclusively between a man and a woman for children. The Church opposes this, not because it opposes gay rights, but because it believes that the common good is best served by restricting marriage to those who fulfil its traditional conditions – the unity of a man and a woman.

Disorder, sin, inclination, act

The language of some Vatican documents describing the homosexual orientation as 'intrinsically disordered' has been wrongly heard as describing gay people themselves. The word is a technical term from moral theology which can sound offensive in the light of the history of homophobic insults. But it is not part of that history; the word is used simply to refer to an inclination away from the purpose and meaning of sex, which is conjugal love (married love open to children). In this sense many inclinations, not just homosexual ones, are 'disordered'. But 'disordered' does not mean 'sinful'. What are sinful are homosexual *acts,* which the *Catechism* describes as 'contrary to the natural law' because they 'close the sexual act to the gift of life' and 'do not proceed from a genuine affective and sexual complementarity'.

All people, whatever their orientation, have a fundamental dignity and are loved by God. We are creatures of desire: some of those desires draw us closer to what is good (ennobling, liberating) for us; others lead us down blind alleys. These latter are 'disordered' desires – including homosexual ones. But that doesn't make them *wrong* in themselves. It is the *actions* which flow from giving into the desires which may be sinful. And those actions are not 'inevitable' as some often claim: we are creatures of desire, but not its prisoners. We are not simply 'driven' by our desires, sexual or otherwise, as if they were some kind of irresistible compulsion. Saying 'no' to some desires is the beginning of morality.

In its 1986 *Letter to the Bishops of the Catholic Church on the Pastoral Care of Homosexual Persons*, the Congregation for the Doctrine of the Faith (CDF) said: 'Although the particular inclination of the homosexual person is not a sin, it is a more or less strong tendency ordered towards an intrinsic moral evil; and thus the inclination itself must be seen as an objective disorder.' It went on to say that it was 'only in the marital relationship that the use of the sexual faculty can be morally good' and that therefore the one who *engages in homosexual behaviour* is acting immorally.

It is not immoral or sinful, in other words, *to be gay*; what are sinful are *homosexual acts*. Explaining the CDF letter, Cardinal Hume's *Note on Church Teaching Concerning Homosexual People* observed that 'the word "disordered" is a harsh one in our English language. It immediately suggests a sinful situation or at least implies a demeaning of the person or even a sickness. It should not be so interpreted.' He added that a homosexual orientation is 'neither morally good nor morally bad; it is homosexual genital acts that are morally wrong'.

Cardinal Hume went on: 'When the Church speaks of the inclination to homosexuality as being 'an objective disorder' the Church can be thinking only of the inclination toward homosexual genital acts. The Church does not consider the whole personality and character of the individual to be thereby disordered. Homosexual people, as well as heterosexual people, can and often do give a fine example of friendship and the art of chaste loving.'

The CDF letter notes: 'To choose someone of the same sex for one's sexual activity is to annul the rich symbolism and meaning, not to mention the goals, of the Creator's sexual design. Homosexual activity is not a complementary union, able to transmit life, and so it thwarts the call to a life of that form of self-giving which the Gospel says is the essence of Christian living. This does not mean that homosexual persons are not often generous and giving of themselves; but when they engage in homosexual activity they confirm within themselves a disordered sexual inclination which is essentially self-indulgent.'

The same letter earlier observes: 'It is only in the marital relationship that the use of the sexual faculty can be morally good.' Sex between a man and a woman, even in marriage, can also be egotistical and self-indulgent. But unlike the gay sexual act, the sexual act between man and woman is *ordered* to self-giving conjugal love, opening the couple to the generosity of accepting new life. That may not be how the sexual act is in fact used, but that is what it is ordered to.

The Church's message to gay people

It can sometimes seem as if the Church simply says 'no' to gay people. What is heard is a series of prohibitions; but there is a more substantial part of the Church's message which goes unheard.

The *Catechism* says gay people 'are called to fulfil God's will in their lives and, if they are Christians, to unite to the sacrifice of the Lord's cross the difficulties they may encounter from their condition.' The Church in this way recognises that living a life of chastity can be a real challenge for a homosexual person, as indeed it is for all those who are not married, whatever their sexual inclination. It can be a call to love and generous self-giving but in a way that is different from the lifelong exclusivity of marriage.'

It goes on: 'By the virtues of self-mastery that teach them inner freedom, at times by the support of disinterested friendship, by prayer and sacramental grace, they can and should gradually and resolutely approach Christian perfection.'

Does that include finding love and fulfilment in a gay relationship? God gives every person the freedom and responsibility to decide how to live their lives. He calls everyone to build loving relationships with other people, and to find fulfilment in genuine friendships. But it is only in marriage, in a lifelong commitment between a man and a woman, that intimacy should involve sex.

Sex is not a basic human need, like food or water; it is not even an essential means of growth and development, like family, community or education. It is not a human right and it is not a necessity. Many, many people, for many different reasons, do not get married, and live chaste lives. They are not less human or happy or fulfilled as a result. They do not love less. Some of the richest, deepest, most fulfilling relationships of friendship are between people of the same sex.

It is a shame that this celibate love, if it is directed towards another of the same gender, is now assumed to be homosexual – conditioned by homoerotic attraction, even if not acted upon. Society is losing the vocabulary to speak about intense friendships between people of the same sex. This makes discussion of this topic hard.

There are many different ways of loving, and forming friendships. But sex has a very particular meaning – to bind a husband and wife together and open their love to the gift of new life. This is the *meaning* of sex. Gay sex is not just an alternative expression of love to heterosexual sex, it is an expression of sexual love that has something missing – namely the possibility of giving new life, and the complementarity of the love between a man and woman. Without that complementarity and openness to life, sex lacks its true purpose.

Existing frame

'The Church is obsessed with sexuality, whether hetero-sexual or gay. If God made people gay, isn't it terrible to condemn them to a life of celibacy? And why does the Church call gay people disordered? The Church's views on contraception are out-dated and it's clear that many prac-tising Catholics, particularly in the West, simply ignore this teaching.'

Reframe

Sexual morality is all about developing our capacity for self-giving love so that we don't use others. The proper context for sex is a lifelong commitment between husband and wife. The Church welcomes and embraces gay people. Many committed Catholics are gay, living faithful and chaste lives. You'll find homosexual people at Mass and working for the Church. The Church rejects discrimination and prejudice against homosexual people. Church teaching does not say homosexual people are disordered, but that sex is ordered to marriage and children, and that is why homosexual people, like all of us who are unmarried, are called to chastity as the best way of learning self-giving love. Of course, marriage may be closed to homosexual people, as it is to many people. But like everyone else who is not married or cannot marry, homosexual people are called to develop intimate, trusting, loving (but chaste) relationships.

Key messages

- Natural family planning (NFP) in its modern form is a means of using a woman's fertility to enable people to plan their families. It is highly effective – both for enabling children, and for spacing them. It involves a couple cooperating – it involves a shared responsibility. It is natural, organic, and respects the body and its cycles, rather than suppressing them.
- Catholics are against artificial contraception because it suppresses fertility rather than regulates it. Not every sexual act will be fertile, but you shouldn't separate sex from its meaning, which is for creating new life and for deepening committed love.

- The 'contraceptive culture' suppresses fertility, and leads to sex being seen as about recreation, not procreation and commitment.
- Sex should be open to children. That is the meaning of it. Sex is a blessing. It is a call to love. But it must be framed within commitment and stability – otherwise the body is lying.
- We favour laws which outlaw discrimination against homosexual people, but not laws which undermine the special place of marriage or which are against the best interests of the child. Cohabiting couples may need protection and support in law with regard to inheritance, tax and other financial issues, but marriage, which can only be between a man and a woman, is a unique institution which deserves special protection, and is the best place for bringing up children.
- The Church does not oppose same-sex marriage and adoption because it is against equality or gay rights, but because other interests and rights (especially those of the child) should weigh more heavily in the balance.

Chapter 3

Equality and religious freedom

Challenging questions:
- Why should the Church be allowed to discriminate against gay people when the law forbids it?
- If Catholic adoption agencies don't want to obey the law, why should they then have access to public funds?
- Why should the Church be allowed to impose its narrow view of the family through taxpayer-funded services?

Legislation banning discrimination against minorities – especially in recent years against gay people – have led, across Europe, to arguments between the Church and governments, and accusations that Catholics are 'opposed to equality', 'seeking the right to discriminate', and failing to grasp a basic tenet of liberal democracy, namely the equality of every individual before the law.

Some of the criticism is prejudiced, raising old ghosts of Catholics as having 'dual loyalties', or of the church trying to 'impose' its view. Some is particularly fierce, especially from gay rights lobbies who see the church as the enemy of what they see as one of the great successes of the modern era, the emancipation of gay people.

The framing of this issue – of a reactionary Church opposing equality – is tragic, given that the equalities ideal is rooted in the basic Christian principle that all are equal in worth and dignity before God. It is also inaccurate in that it supposes that 'equality' is a fixed notion, something people either believe in or not. In reality, equality is a strongly contested political notion, in that it raises questions of values and rights. ('The worst form of inequality is to try to make unequal things equal,' said Aristotle.)

While the Church is strongly against, in principle, unjust discrimination against minorities, not everything that someone might regard as 'discrimination' the Church would agree to be so. The same is true of rights. As we saw in the last chapter, the Church does not believe, for example, in the 'right of gay people to marry', because it believes that marriage is designed for a man and a woman, for the sake of children. Indeed, the question of whether same-sex couples should have 'the right to marry' is really a question of whether a same-sex 'marriage' is equal to the marriage of a man and a woman, or whether – given that marriage is a social institution, above all designed for the nurturing of children – other rights are involved.

'Discrimination' is considered a bad thing, and in arguments over cases such as the adoption agencies, Catholics often find themselves accused of asking for the 'freedom to discriminate', like a hotel which refuses black families. But this is an absurdly unjust frame. 'Discrimination' means separating or excluding for irrational or prejudiced reasons; where the exclusion is reasonable, the result of weighing other reasonable rights in the balance, it is not discrimination. Thus the law prohibits racially segregated public toilets, but not public toilets segregated by gender. The first is discriminatory, but not the second. In the first case, the motivation is irrational prejudice (there can be no other reason for racially dividing toilets); in the second the motive is the recognition of legitimately differing needs and rights: it is 'reasonable', and not discriminatory, for men to be excluded from women's toilets and vice versa.

The 'equalities' agenda should not be driven by an attempt to give everything and everybody an equivalent legal status, but by the need to remove barriers to participation in society, democracy and the economy by all. It is reasonable to distinguish in law between the natural institution of marriage, entered into by a man and a woman in part for procreation, and other forms of union, which are not 'equal' (in that they do not serve the same social good) and therefore do not call for the same protection and encouragement by the law.

The other neuralgic issue concerns the way such laws are implemented. Giving 'equality' to one group in society can seriously prejudice the rights and interests of another group. The Church is a passionate advocate of the general principle of curbing discrimination – that no one should be allowed in law to refuse to employ or offer a service to someone on the grounds of their race, gender or disability. The disagreements arise over *how* those equality laws are implemented. And behind that clash are different perceptions of a liberal and pluralistic society.

Sometimes laws are proposed or enacted which directly affect the Church's 'natural' freedoms and rights, or which seek to coerce Catholics in a way that violates their conscience. This goes against the principle that the law should be applied wherever possible in a way that accommodates minorities, a principle that goes back to the nineteenth century, when laws were introduced to protect minorities from the effects of laws enacted for the majority. Thus Jews, Catholics and Protestant dissenters were permitted to take oaths in non-Anglican ceremonies, which freed them to marry and take seats in Parliament. In the modern era, allowing Sikh motorcyclists to wear turbans instead of crash helmets, or allowing Catholic doctors not to perform abortions are classic examples of the accommodation of minorities on the basis of conscience. Catholics strongly disagreed with the 1967 Abortion Act, and have continued to argue against it. The law respects that disagreement. In the NHS a Catholic doctor is free in law to refuse to perform abortions.

The law, in other words, balances the majority view that a woman is free to choose an abortion with the recognition that a Catholic is free in conscience not to have to carry one out. The law is the law; and all are equal before it. But it is *applied differently* to different groups. This is an essential principle in the equalities project. Minorities need sometimes to be protected from the effects of a law. They are not being allowed to 'opt out' of the law: they remain fully subject to it. But the law treats them differently.

Allowing such exemptions is crucial to a healthy coexistence in a pluralistic society. It is also necessary in a democracy which allows the freedom of faith alongside the freedom of other faiths or secular beliefs. Disagreements between Church and governments over this issue do not indicate a reactionary Church in conflict with a liberal state – the usual frame. They are really about two models of a liberal society, in which the Church's model has the stronger liberal credentials, reflecting a deeper, richer pluralism, as opposed to a narrower, individualist model of liberal democracy.

Modern democracies separate Church and state in the sense that states are not 'confessional': they do not seek to impose Christian beliefs on people, as happens in theocracies. But this does not mean they should be 'secular theocracies', coercing Christians into acting against their consciences by imposing beliefs contrary to those convictions. As a rule, the state should reflect the variety of beliefs in society and seek to enact laws which are sensitive to the needs and rights of those diverse groups.

This is an example of what some in the Church call a 'positive secularism' – namely, a religiously and ideologically neutral state which respects and understands the needs and rights of faith. What the Church objects to as undemocratic is what Pope Benedict XVI calls 'aggressive secularism', in which the state fails to recognise the natural freedoms and rights of the Church in the public square, reducing religion to a merely private matter, in which the Church is treated as an association of like-minded individuals rather than, as should be the case, a 'natural society' with its intrinsic freedoms and rights.

At the heart of this issue, then, is a question of weighing two essential freedoms: equality (or 'freedom from discrimination') with freedom of religion. A modern democratic European state is bound by the European Convention on Human Rights (EHCR) to balance them. A law which exaggerates one freedom at the expense of the other is a bad law.

Article 9 of the ECHR, entrenched in UK law via the Human Rights Act 1998, notes that 'freedom of religion or beliefs shall be subject only to such limitations as are prescribed by law and necessary in a democratic society in the interests of public safety, for the protection of public order, health or morals, or the protection of the rights and freedoms of others.' That is a high bar: the burden is on the law-makers to demonstrate the necessity of curbing religious freedom for one of those reasons.

What is freedom of religion? A key element of it is that charities and religious bodies should be free to 'manifest belief', namely, to create organisations inspired by and witnessing to their religious ethos. That means selecting certain kinds of people to run them, and having policies and practices which witness to the values underpinning them. Faith-based organisations must be free to be consistent with their beliefs by the way they act – as long as they do not offend public order or inhibit the rights and freedoms of others. This freedom is much larger and more contentious than the 'freedom of worship'. It is also vital to civil society, which is nurtured and sustained by such value-driven organisations.

Neither equality nor religious freedom is limitless. Equality is not an absolute; nor is religious freedom. The common good of society calls for limits on both. But the common good also calls for those limits to be kept in balance. This has become harder in recent years because of the prevalence of a secular liberal mentality which sees only individuals, not the organisations and associations which connect them. The belief that rights are essentially assertions of individual autonomies has led governments to exaggerate the first (equality) while failing to grasp the significance of the second (religious freedom). As Pope Benedict in January 2010 told the bishops of England and Wales: 'Your country is well known for its firm commitment to equality of opportunity for all members of society. Yet … the effect of some of the legislation designed to achieve this goal has been to impose unjust limitations on the freedom of religious communities to act in accordance with their beliefs.'

Positive intention

The positive intention in this argument is underpinned by the belief that in a modern pluralistic society we should all be equal before the law and have equal rights regardless of race, religion, gender, sexual orientation or disability. Legislation has rightly been put in place to ensure this. So it seems clearly right and just, for example, that a wheelchair-user should have as equal access as an able-bodied person to public buildings. Or that a woman cannot be fired from her job simply because she is pregnant. Or that a white candidate should not be preferred to a black candidate during a job interview simply on grounds of race. The positive intention behind the criticism of the Church's opposition to, say, same-sex adoption appeals to the core Christian principle of the equal dignity and worth of every human being, and the historic Gospel task of emancipating those who have been marginalised and excluded.

Upholding marriage

The marriage of a man and woman is a unique kind of human relationship, the only one capable of bringing forth a child to be brought up by a mother and father who have made a public commitment to one another. Evidence overwhelmingly points to the benefits of children being raised by their biological parents in a stable, committed, publicly sanctioned partnership. That is why society has traditionally given special support and recognition to marriage, the only form of human relationship which is also an institution. As an institution, it has certain rights, benefits as well as obligations; both Church and state set a series of conditions for entering it. To bar others from it (those unwilling to make a commitment, for example; or people of the same sex) is not discrimination; it is designed to preserve what makes that institution special, for the benefit of the whole of society.

Despite many pressures on it, and frequent breakdowns, marriage remains an impressive social good, producing a broad range of beneficial outcomes to both individuals and society as a whole. Children brought up in intact married homes are far less likely to suffer poverty, abuse, ill-health, addiction, disadvantage at school and work – and are much less likely to become divorced or unwed parents themselves.

Marriage, in other words, is an essentially pro-child institution. Children of course are brought up in many other contexts – by cohabiting or same-sex couples, for example – but those contexts are not protected by the law in the same way, because they are less beneficial to children, and can harm their interests. When the

Church opposes same-sex marriage and adoption, therefore, it is 'discriminating' only in the sense that it favours the state maintaining a legitimate distinction between the institution of marriage and other forms of partnership by upholding, protecting, and encouraging marriage through the law; and does so, essentially, because it believes that this is in the best interests of children.

The civil society principle

Religious freedom is not a small matter for the Church – or for society as a whole. As one of the leading actors in civil society – running a large network of schools, clinics, charities, and so on – it understands the importance of religious motivation. People set up, work for and give their lives to church organisations because their faith inspires them; feeling grateful for the gifts of God, being people of compassion and sensitive to the needs of the world, and often fired by a strong sense of social justice and civic commitment, they establish schools, homeless shelters, child welfare charities, adoption agencies, hospices and countless other projects and institutes tackling addiction, family breakdown, and poverty in all its forms. The Catholic Church is a remarkable contributor to the common good in this respect (see Chapter 1).

Nor are these Catholic organisations at the service only of other Catholics: they serve the whole of society, addressing the needs of people whatever their beliefs or backgrounds. The result is that Catholic civil organisations make a massive contribution to the common good of the UK, worth many tens of millions of pounds. The most high-profile examples are the Church's many and

popular schools (see Chapter 6). That is why the 'freedom to manifest belief' is so essential to a healthy civil
society. Without the freedom to witness to the values of
the Gospel and the teachings of the Catholic Church –
what is usually described as a 'Catholic ethos' – these
organisations would shrivel and die, or become empty
shells, to the detriment of all. When Government talks
about the 'Big Society', by which it means a vigorous civil
society, it is recognising the importance of inspiration
and motivation. But the corollary of the Big Society is
religious freedom. You can't have the fruits without the
roots.

Laws which seek to free people from discrimination –
in themselves a worthy objective, applauded by the
Church – must take care that they don't restrict the
freedom to manifest belief which is vital to the flourishing of these organisations. It is wrong, in principle, for an
actively homosexual person (in a civil partnership, say) to
be denied a job simply on the grounds of that orientation,
where that orientation is not remotely relevant to the job
– as an accountant, say. But if that person applies to be
the principal of a Catholic school, it *is* relevant, because
the Church teaches that active homosexuality is wrong,
and the principal of a Catholic school is responsible for
witnessing to, and upholding, the ethos of the school. An
anti-discrimination law which made it illegal for a school
to 'discriminate' in this way would quickly undermine its
ethos, and therefore its *raison d'être*.

On the whole, laws banning discrimination keep this
in mind: a school has the freedom in law – often in the
form of an exemption – to prefer a married Catholic to a
Catholic in a civil partnership in the job application

process. But in recent years there has been a greater reluctance by Government to grant such exemptions.

Do such exemptions adversely affect others? No, because people have a choice about which school they apply to be a teacher in; or they can choose between different suppliers of particular goods and services. If the only schools were Catholic schools, of course, it would be a different matter. But there are many more non-Catholic schools than Catholic ones.

It is also important, of course, for the 'discrimination' in these cases to be reasonable, or what the Church would call 'just'. A woman responsible for cleaning the classrooms does not need to be a Catholic, or leading a lifestyle consistent with a Catholic ethos, because her job does not involve per se setting an example or witnessing. In the same way, respect for religious freedom does not mean accommodating any preference dressed up as conviction, or which a religious group claims to be religious. But in matters relating to issues of central concern across religious traditions, issues touching on the meaning of human life and death, the Government is obliged to accommodate deeply held mainstream religious convictions as long as these do not significantly damage anyone.

Yet this delicate balancing act in law – the job of Parliament – has often gone wrong in recent years as laws are enacted which fail to recognise the importance of the freedom of religion. Because of the growing secularisation of the governing classes – shown in a lack of empathy or understanding among some politicians for what makes faith organisations tick – there have been clashes with the Church over some recent equality laws.

The most significant in the UK in recent years was legislation enacted in 2007 which resulted in the closure of the Catholic Church's 13 adoption agencies.

The adoption agencies: a wake-up call

In April 2007 the Government passed a series of regulations prohibiting discrimination against homosexual and lesbian people in the supply of goods and services, known as the Equality Act (Sexual Orientation) Regulations 2007, or 'SORs'. The Act made it illegal, for example, for a hotel to refuse to provide a double room to a same-sex couple. But the SORs applied not just to businesses but also to charities and voluntary organisations. And they classified adoption as one of those goods and services.

Catholic adoption agencies, responsible for a third of all placements of children by voluntary agencies, had an enviable record in placing children with parents. In 2004–05, they placed 227 children and approved 176 adopters, and had the lowest disruption rates (when a child, having been placed with a parent, later has to return to care) of any group of agencies, less than 4 per cent in comparison with 8 per cent (other voluntary agencies) and 10 per cent (local authorities). The Catholic agencies believed that this success related, in part, to their belief that marriage offered the best and most stable environment for an adopted child to grow up in.

The agencies had known for more than a year they would be in the firing line of the new law: other European countries implementing the same European directive had not defined adoption as a service, but in the UK the inclusion of adoption had been a key demand of the gay rights lobby to which the Government acquiesced. The adoption agencies knew what this meant: they were going to be legally obliged to consider same-sex couples as adoptive parents in the same way that they considered a man – woman couple or a single person, or face being taken to court for discrimination.

But opening up their adoption service to same-sex couples was also unthinkable. The Church has made some strong comments in the past about same-sex adoption. It considers that same-sex adoption is not in a child's best interests because it denies them the gift of a mother and father who would take the place of their own natural parents. Marriage, and the love of a mother and father, are the best forms of family life for a growing child.

Proving this is not always easy. The psychological impact of same-sex adoption on children remains warmly debated by psychologists, and the best that can be said is that the jury is out on the matter.

What are not in doubt are the statistics on stability. Children born into married unions are twice as likely as those born to cohabiting couples to spend their childhoods with their natural parents; the figures for cohabiting same-sex couples are even worse than those for cohabiting heterosexual couples, fewer than one in ten of whom are still together after ten years. Nor is there much doubt that same-sex adoption reduces the number of relationship role-models, depriving a child of the male – female relationship, a mother and father coordinating parenting, and either a father – child or a mother – child relationship.

Yet same-sex adoption has been legal in the UK for many years. The issue in 2006 was not solely, or even mainly, an issue about whether same-sex parents offer as good an environment for children as other kinds of parents. It was about the freedom of an adoption agency to decide on that question for themselves. There was another key freedom at stake: the freedom to take a stand in promoting the value and importance of marriage, which is no longer the bedrock of society. This is a good example of a Catholic ethos – to be a sign of contradiction in modern society, to point to values which are being eroded or undermined. For the Catholic adoption agencies, it was key to their *raison d'être*. They needed an exemption from the SORs in order to carry on being themselves.

The Archbishop of Westminster at the time, Cardinal Cormac Murphy-O'Connor, told the Cabinet it would be 'unreasonable, unnecessary and unjust discrimination against Catholics for the Government to insist that if they wish to continue to work with local authorities, Catholic adoption agencies must act against the teaching of the Church and their own consciences by being obliged in law to provide such a service.' At the same time, the Cardinal made clear, the Church 'utterly condemns all forms of unjust discrimination, violence, harassment or abuse directed against people who are homosexual' and said the Church recognised many elements of recent legislation which banned such discrimination.

The letter failed to persuade the Cabinet. Those in favour of the exemption were voted down, and the SORs went through Parliament in their original form.

Although, at the time of writing, a legal case brought by one of the agencies is still underway, the result has been that the Catholic adoption services have either closed, or severed their links to the Church. Some of them date back to the eighteenth century. A crucial witness – as well as a vital service to British society – was lost.

Adoption agencies: the arguments

Advocates of the SORs – above all the gay rights lobby – argued that refusing gay people the right to adopt was to restrict their freedom in law; yet same-sex couples have for many years had the right in law to adopt, and had long sought to exercise that right in the country's 400 council-run agencies, without that right being restricted by the refusal of 13 agencies to consider them as parents. As Cardinal Murphy-O'Connor pointed out in his letter, the Catholic agencies took seriously their duty to refer same-sex couples to 'other agencies where their adoption application may be considered'.

Some argued that if a law prohibited discrimination one could not have exceptions to that law on principle. Yet anti-discrimination laws have often been enacted – as we showed above – with exemptions for charities and faith-based organisations. Others argued that the agencies were in receipt of public funds, and that the condition for public funding was that a service had to be equally open to all. But again, there are many instances – faith schools, for example – where that principle has never been applied, because the other 'good' involved (preserving the ethos) counterbalances it.

Some appealed to the example of anti-racist or gender-equality laws achieving over time the eradication of racist or sexist attitudes. Should the law allow an agency to refuse a black couple, by appealing to some passage of Scripture? But that comparison was odious. That would be an example of 'unjust' discrimination, of irrational prejudice rather than reasonable conviction.

The justification for refusing the exemption essentially came down to a view which alarmed the bishops: that the Church was 'homophobic' and that the law was a means of forcing the Church either to adopt a more 'progressive' attitude or pay the price. It was a means, in other words, of using the law to coerce the Church into altering its teaching, in much the same way as the law might be used to coerce people into renouncing racist or anti-social behaviour.

Yet to refuse a same-sex couple the right to adopt was not irrational prejudice; it arose from a deep-seated conviction about the nature of the family which has long been the bedrock of human society. Many nowadays disagree that the 'traditional family' is in any way preferable to alternatives (same-sex, single-parent, etc.); but was the state really now declaring that it was 'irrational prejudice' to believe otherwise?

For the adoption agencies to refuse to consider gay couples was no more discriminatory than refusing an elderly couple the right to adopt. The policy did not reflect hostility to gay couples or the elderly, but a view about what was best for children.

There is no 'right to adopt' in the European Convention on Human Rights (EHCR). The process of selecting adoptive parents is, essentially, about agencies discerning what is right for children. The long experience of the Catholic adoption agencies, reinforced by the faith which led to their founding, was that children's interests were best served by actively preferring stable, married, male – female role-models which, they argued, made for the most stable, healthy upbringing. The policy, in other words, was informed by a desire to advocate positively for the model of family sanctioned by the Christian, and indeed almost every other, faith and by the conviction that this model best served the interests of the children.

But there was another worrying dimension to the closure of the adoption agencies: a highly controversial notion of the state. The Church saw in the implementation of the SORs an assumption that the state acts on society in order to condition it – to impose a certain ideological view, in this case of the family. It also implied a model of society in which there is no such thing as 'intermediate associations', only individuals, families and the state. In the traditional Christian understanding, people belong not just to families but have other, wider allegiances – to communities of value, with different moral narratives. A nation, in this vision, is a 'community of communities'. It is the state's task to regulate the relationships between these communities, to prevent them accumulating powers which prevent other communities from flourishing; it is not the state's task to impose an ideological narrative. But in the individualist liberal conception of state and society, there is nothing but a state and many individuals; therefore, one moral narrative – in this case, that same-sex couples are equal to traditional couples – must prevail.

In the case of the adoption agencies, Parliament was telling the Church that its organisations must accept the principle that same-sex couples are equal to the traditional family, and that this principle trumps their freedom to continue to advocate otherwise. This is what Pope Benedict memorably called the 'dictatorship of relativism', which is as illiberal as the theocratic principle that the only form of union recognised by the state is Christian marriage. Ironically, therefore, the Church – often accused of opposing liberal values – has become sometimes a lonely advocate of a core liberal principle.

This ideological view of the state contradicts a key element of the Catholic understanding of the public square. It is not the state's task to condition the consciences of its people, but to regulate and balance different rights and freedoms. This argument was not about the freedom of religious organisations to 'discriminate'; it was about whether the state should be allowed to interfere with religious organisations and to impose on them certain ideologies. Through the SORs the Government was telling civil-society organisations that if they wished to exist, and receive public funding, they must adhere to an ideological view that same-sex families are just as good for children and for society as the traditional family. That message sent a chill down the spines of the leaders not just of the Catholic Church but of other Churches and faith organisations – and helped to frame the agenda for the papal visit of September 2010.

Throughout his visit, Pope Benedict XVI made the case for political pluralism to be dependent on religious freedom. Speaking to political leaders at Westminster Hall (17 September 2010), he said that 'religious bodies – including institutions linked to the Catholic Church – need to be free to act in accordance with their own principles and specific convictions based upon the faith and the official teaching of the Church. In this way, such basic rights as religious freedom, freedom of conscience and freedom of association are guaranteed.'

The existing frame

'The Catholic Church, like other Christian bodies, has a retrograde, homophobic and irrational view of homosexuality which is out of step with progressive, liberal values of tolerance. It uses its power and resources to lobby the Government to be allowed to disobey the law in order to continue to promote its homophobia. All organisations should operate within the law, and no organisation, particularly one in receipt of public money, should be allowed to continue to promote its divisive, intolerant views or to continue to discriminate against the gay minority.'

Reframe

The Catholic Church is one of the world's leading advocates of equality and human rights, and believes nobody should be subject to unjust discrimination. This issue is not about the right to discriminate, but about the balance of freedoms in a modern pluralistic society – the need for some groups to be free from discrimination, and the freedom to form organisations and witness to their beliefs. It is about whether or not equality laws reflect that proper balance. The Church is not asking to be exempt from the law; it is asking for the law to be implemented differently for different groups, as happens already in many laws, in order to preserve a greater good. A healthy civil society hinges on the freedom of faith-based and other organisa-

*tions with strong values to create and run those organisa-
tions in accordance with those values, as long as they don't
inhibit other people's freedoms. When the SORs were
implemented, the power of the state was used to coerce
Catholic adoption agencies into conforming to a view of
the family at odds with Christian belief. The closure of the
agencies showed that the concept of pluralism is at risk in
the UK.*

Key messages

- The modern principle of equality has its roots in the Christian principle that all people are of equal value; this principle underlies the abolition of the slave trade and the civil rights movements of the 1960s. The Catholic Church is globally one of the leading advocates of equality and rights – for the elderly, the unborn, immigrants, women and gay people. The Church does not oppose equality, but finds itself opposed to the way equality laws are sometimes implemented in the modern era in ways that negatively affect other rights and freedoms.

- Protecting minorities from unjust discrimination is one of the major tasks of the modern state. They remain fully subject to the law, but the law treats them differently.

- Government has moved in the last 20 years beyond protecting minorities from the negative consequences of laws designed for the majority, to developing laws designed for the minorities themselves. A vital principle here is even-handedness: governments must take care not to introduce a hierarchy of rights in which one community is favoured over another.

- When the Church asks for exemptions, it is not trying to condition the law in accordance with its beliefs ('imposing its views') but appealing to a well-established principle in modern democracy and European rights legislation – the need to protect, in law, the freedom to associate and to manifest belief, which is the key principle behind the 'Big Society'. The corollary of a vigorous civil society is religious freedom.
- The Church's advocacy of marriage as an institution deserving of protection by the state, stems from the unique nature of marriage as beneficial to children and to society in general. Excluding from it those who do not meet its essential conditions is not discrimination but an attempt to preserve its unique nature.

Chapter 4

Euthanasia and assisted suicide

> **Challenging questions**
> - *Why does the Church oppose allowing people to choose the time of their own death?*
> - *If a person of sound mind who is terminally ill and in dreadful pain wishes to die, why should the law prevent them by prosecuting those who assist them?*
> - *Doctors have always helped people on their way to death; how is legally assisted suicide any different?*
> - *What right does the Church have to tell people of no faith how they should end their lives?*
> - *Society is changing its mind about assisted dying, as opinion polls show. Isn't this another case of the Church trying to legislate for everyone else?*

The drive to make it legal to help someone commit suicide is one of the principal – perhaps *the* principal – ethical debates of our time, comparable, in its way, to the debate over legalising abortion in the 1960s. So far in the UK it remains illegal to enable someone to end his or her life, either by someone handing a person the lethal drugs he or she self-administers (known as 'assisted suicide'), or a doctor administering those same drugs in order to cause death (known as 'voluntary euthanasia'). The pressure on Parliament to follow the examples of a handful of

European countries and make it legal in the UK grows greater all the time, following a series of high-profile, emotive campaigns and TV programmes which powerfully appeal for the right to be free of unnecessary suffering.

The case in favour is at heart one of personal autonomy: if a person is suffering unbearably, and wishes to end their life at a particular point, and in the manner of their choosing, who has any right to stop them? Yet the question is not about the legality of suicide, which is not a crime (but nor is it a right), but about the legality of bringing about another's suicide, which raises a large number of other issues.

The drive to allow assisted suicide arises in part from modern advances in medical technology. An ageing population means a greater prevalence of long-term, terminal conditions such as motor-neurone disease, Parkinson's and Alzheimer's, which bring about great changes in a person and undoubted suffering. A man or woman nowadays faces years of debilitating illness and suffering in a way that would have been unknown in previous eras.

Such conditions often mean the loss of capacities and abilities which a person has set great store by. A high-profile campaigner for an assisted suicide law, the best-selling novelist Terry Pratchett, fears that his Alzheimer's will one day mean he can no longer write. That moment, he said on a TV documentary in June 2011, would mean for him 'the end' – one he would rather avoid by swallowing barbiturates.

Such feelings are understandable, and common. In a high-achieving society, people build their egos and satisfaction around their successes and powers. But are lives less worth living once these vanish?

Whatever an individual may conclude, are we as a society prepared to endorse that idea? And what effect would that have on the way society views the elderly – or indeed the poor, the disabled and the unsuccessful?

The playwright and eugenicist George Bernard Shaw said in 1934: 'The moment we face it frankly we are driven to the conclusion that the community has a right to put a price on the right to live in it … If people are fit to live, let them live under decent human conditions. If they are not fit to live, kill them in a decent human way.'

Advocates of legalising euthanasia reject the comparison with the eugenicists of the 1920s and 30s who paved the way for the Nazi death camps; where eugenicists favoured *compulsory* sterilisation, abortion and euthanasia, the modern case for assisted dying rests, like that of abortion, on the 'right to choose': it is for the individual to decide, coolly and with forethought, the manner and time of his or her death. As Pratchett put it in a speech in February 2010: 'It seems to me quite a reasonable and sensible decision for someone with a serious, incurable and debilitating disease to elect for a medically assisted death by appointment.'

But while such a choice may seem to that individual 'reasonable', is it reasonable or desirable for the law to sanction such a choice? As with abortion, therefore, the argument is about the extent to which personal autonomy should trump other considerations. With assisted suicide, of course, the aim is to end one's own life, not that of another (the child in the womb), so the personal autonomy case seems more compelling. Yet it is a fallacy to suppose that in a decision like this a decision can ever be 'individual'. Suicide has a profound impact on others. Our lives are interconnected in countless ways. Allowing for the exercise of autonomy in this case would rapidly alter the conditions for others in society.

Positive intention

There are many positive values in the case for legalising assisted suicide. It is compassionate to seek to help someone suffering serious pain to be free of it. Many of the high-profile cases of people who have gone to die in Switzerland's dying clinics describe people suffering despair linked to their condition over many years, and others who cannot endure the loss of some faculty to which their sense of self was closely tied. Daniel James, the 23-year-old rugby player who was left paralysed from the chest down after a sporting accident said he preferred death to a second-class existence; the 59-year-old retired professor who went to Zurich five months after being diagnosed with motor-neurone disease, said assisted death was an alternative to 'utter hell'. These are people whose view of their lives has been altered by suffering, to the point that what they endure obliterates everything else. The only possible response to such stories is compassion and sympathy.

There is a positive intention, too, behind those who point to the many failings in the way the dying are treated in hospitals, sometimes with inadequate pain

> *relief, or poorly cared for. The experience of seeing someone you love endure inadequate care can produce a horror of dying.*

Why the Church opposes euthanasia

In common with a longstanding tradition of western civilisation, the Church believes that dying naturally is a vital part of life's journey, in many ways the most meaningful part. Dying can be described as a process of healing: important things happen on that journey, and suffering and pain may be a part of it. As the Archbishop of Westminster, Vincent Nichols, said in 2010, 'For those of our faith, this is the moment when, whether we are weak and struggling, tranquil and awake, or in some other inner space, we hand ourselves over to our loving Father. This moment is central to our pilgrim journey. We practise for it, day by day, rehearsing our final act of trust with smaller daily acts of abandonment to God, in prayer, in kindness towards others, and in our sacramental life.'

Abandonment, in other words, is a gradual process of renunciation which is highly meaningful to the one who undergoes it. Although some die swiftly and painlessly, very often the pattern of dying involves great suffering, because (and this is true of old age in general) it means renouncing all those things which in our lives we believe make us worthwhile and loveable: our looks, intelligence, abilities and capabilities. This is what the great Swiss psychiatrist Carl Jung called 'necessary suffering', the suffering endured by the ego, which protests at having to change. The idea that this kind of suffering is part of growth is not a uniquely 'religious' view, although Christianity – with the cross and the resurrection at its heart – has perhaps a richer theological understanding than most secular outlooks

And yet while the Church urges the need to accept necessary suffering, it vigorously opposes what might be called 'unnecessary suffering'. The abandonment and renunciation of illness and dying require loving support. Excessive physical pain, and the loneliness of abandonment, can and should be avoided. That is why it is church organisations, pioneered in the UK by the Christian hospice movement founded by Dame Cicely Saunders, that have transformed the way society now cares for the dying. 'Last days are not … lost days,' she declared. Rather than seeing themselves as burdensome and unwanted, people with terminal illness should be in circles of love and care where they will be valued and made comfortable. The Church's view is that hospices need to be extended and made more accessible, such that no one ever needs to die alone and in severe pain. Hospices meet the needs of the dying much better than hospitals, which are not geared to those who no longer need treatment: where hospitals 'cure', hospices 'care'.

This is not, it should be clear, about extending a life unnecessarily. It is not right zealously to provide burdensome treatment to extend a life when it is disproportionate to the relief it brings. Pain management – the specialism of hospice care – may sometimes shorten a life. If the intention is not to kill but to alleviate suffering, even when death is a foreseen result of that intervention, that is not euthanasia. The purpose of palliative care is to provide an environment of love and support for a person on their final journey.

Still, no amount of palliative care will convince those who argue that dying is devoid of any intrinsic meaning (which, without God and an afterlife, it arguably is); who don't think death has any purpose beyond ending life; and for whom the indignity associated with the process should at all costs be avoided, whether or not it involves intense suffering. Advocates of a change in the law see this is as a classic case of religious people trying to impose their own norms on other people through the coercive power of the state. And anyway, they argue, nothing they propose prevents anyone choosing, if they wish, to die a 'natural' death.

But the Church's opposition to assisted dying is not an attempt to persuade people of no faith to adopt a religious view of death. Nor does it appeal to the right to die a natural death. The Church's opposition relies on a view of the common good of society, and how legalising assisted suicide would undermine that good.

The law cannot, in reality, be neutral; giving people the 'right to die' would immediately and profoundly affect the way society viewed dying. If participating in a suicide is legally and ethically acceptable it can only be because there's a *right* to suicide; once we allow that such a right exists, the arguments for confining it to the dying seem arbitrary at best. In the same way, choosing to allow God or nature to take its course would over time come to be regarded as optional, eccentric and even selfish.

As the Archbishop of Canterbury put it in 2010: 'The freedom of one person to utilise in full consciousness a legal provision for assisted suicide brings with it a risk to the freedom of others not to be manipulated or harassed or simply demoralised when in a weakened condition.'

Once the possibility of legal assisted dying were conceded in law, he went on, it would 'create an ethical framework in which the worthwhileness of some lives is undermined by the legal expression of what feels like public impatience with protracted dying and "unproductive" lives'.

Some context

Physician-assisted suicide (PAS) is legal for the terminally ill in the US states of Oregon (1997) and Washington (2008). PAS and physician-administered euthanasia (PAE) have been legal in the Netherlands since 2001; PAE only in Belgium since 2002. Switzerland legalised assisted suicide as long ago as 1942, but this was not in the context of clinical illness (assisted suicide is not regarded in Switzerland as a medical procedure). In England and Wales the pressure is to legalise PAS only, in Scotland both PAS and PAE. The advocates claim, naturally, that experience of legalisation overseas demonstrates that it works well; opponents point to the same experience to argue the opposite.

At the time of an attempt by Lord Joffe to introduce an assisted dying bill in 2004–05, a select committee of the House of Lords under the chairmanship of former Lord Chancellor Lord Mackay of Clashfern conducted an exhaustive study of the subject, taking expert evidence from over 140 witnesses in four jurisdictions: the UK, Oregon, the Netherlands and Switzerland. It received over 60 formal submissions from relevant organisations, including the Catholic Bishops' Conference of England and Wales, and more than 14,000 letters and emails from members of the public. Lord Joffe's bill and the committee ran out of time before the 2005 General Election. But the Committee still reported on the evidence it had received and on what it considered to be shortcomings in Lord Joffe's bill which it said would need to be addressed in the event of it coming again before Parliament.

The report drew attention to two important points. First, that underpinning calls for a change in the law was a demand for personal autonomy that was largely irrelevant to the degree of suffering involved. The Lords noted: 'It is clear to us from the evidence we have received that the demand for assisted suicide or voluntary euthanasia is particularly strong among determined individuals whose suffering derives more from the fact of their terminal illness than from its symptoms and who are unlikely to be deflected from their wish to end their lives by more or better palliative care.' Second, experience from other countries suggested 'a strong link between the scope of legislation in this area and its take-up by terminally ill people. In particular, where legislation is limited to assistance with suicide, the take-up rate is dramatically less than in places where voluntary euthanasia is also legalised.'

The UK law as it stands

Suicide was decriminalised by the 1961 Suicide Act, so people who attempt to take their own lives are not prosecuted if they fail: in fact, they are rushed to hospital and offered clinical and psychological help. But helping another to commit suicide remains a criminal offence under Section 2 of the Act and is punishable on conviction by a maximum of 14 years' imprisonment. In decriminalising suicide 50 years ago Parliament was clear that it did not wish to signal that suicide was an acceptable act to be approved or encouraged; and it remained intent on keeping assisting suicide illegal because of the danger that people with malicious motives could justify killing others or pressuring them into killing themselves. The law exists, in other words, to protect the vulnerable (the elderly, disabled, the ill) from coercion.

There is no law specifically prohibiting euthanasia – that is, the killing of one person by another for compassionate reasons. Acts of euthanasia, where they occur, are classed as murder or manslaughter depending on the circumstances.

But prosecutions are rare. Every case of assisted suicide or euthanasia is investigated on its merits and the relevant evidence examined. If pressure has been brought to bear on the victim or if the suspect acted from a desire for personal gain, prosecution can result. If the motives of the one assisting are purely compassionate – the victim has suffered from a serious illness, pleading persistently for assistance, which was given reluctantly and after much thought – prosecution is usually not considered to be in the public interest.

Yet the deterrent effect of the present law ensures that very few cases of 'assisted dying' occur. The threat of penalties ensures that anyone who is contemplating assisting another with suicide must think very carefully indeed before doing so. As a result the cases that come before the Crown Prosecution Service (CPS) are usually extreme in nature, and unlikely to result in prosecution. Over the past 10 years, none of the 120 or so 'Swiss' assisted suicide cases – when a British man or woman wanting to die has been accompanied by relatives to the Dignitas euthanasia service in Zurich – has resulted in prosecution. Campaigners for a change in the law argue that this proves that the law needs to be changed. Yet the fact that prosecutions barely ever happen is not a reason for changing the law but a good reason for not doing so.

If euthanasia were allowed, the evidence from Holland and Oregon suggests that the numbers of assisted suicide cases would rapidly increase, and most would not be of the extreme nature that currently appear before the British courts: a study in *The Journal of Medical Ethics* suggested that 21 per cent of the people whom Dignitas helps to commit suicide – more than 1,000 in the past 15 years – are not terminally ill. And around 60 per cent of more than 130 suicides Dr Jack Kevorkian assisted weren't actually terminally ill. The dark logic of assisted suicide is incapable of distinguishing types of suffering.

As the Archbishop of Canterbury has put it: 'the balance of liberties still comes out against a new legal framework, and in favour of holding to the principle – not that life should be prolonged at all costs, but that the legal initiating of a process whose sole or main purpose is to end life is again to cross a moral boundary, and to enter some very dangerous territory in practical terms. Most of us would still hold that the current state of the law, with all its discretionary powers and nuances about degrees of culpability in extreme cases, serves us better than an opening of the door into provision for the legal ending of lives.'

The absence of prosecutions has been used by campaigners to argue that to see this system of 'forgiveness' should be replaced with a formal procedure for licensing death in advance in accord with a 'check list' of conditions.

Yet we do not license other criminal offences in advance; the decision to prosecute depends on the severity of the offence and the circumstances surrounding each case. Why should 'assisted dying' be treated differently? There is also a *practical* objection. A licence granted for assisted suicide does not have to be acted on as soon as it is granted; in Oregon many months can elapse before a successful applicant decides to swallow prescribed lethal drugs, and may have changed his or her mind in the interim. Yet the licence is for the one assisting; what is to prevent that person mixing the prescribed lethal drugs into the victim's food without his or her knowledge and claiming after the event that death resulted from the victim's own action?

In 2008–09 Debbie Purdy, a multiple sclerosis sufferer, petitioned first the High Court, then the Court of Appeal and finally the House of Lords (now the Supreme Court) to instruct the Director of Public Prosecutions (DPP) to clarify the grounds for prosecution of those who assist in a suicide. She wanted it made clear under what circumstances her husband would be prosecuted, in the event that he accompanied her at some future date to Switzerland, to seek assisted suicide at the Dignitas suicide clinic. What Purdy was seeking was complete assurance that, provided he complied with certain requirements in assisting her suicide, her husband would not be prosecuted. Her petition was eventually (July 2009) upheld by the House of Lords, and the DPP was instructed to publish prosecution guidelines.

The DPP did so in February 2010 after widespread consultation. The final guidelines make no distinction on grounds of the state of health the victim or the relationship of the victim to the assister, and they stipulate that assisted suicide given by a doctor or health-care professional will be regarded as an aggravating factor in deciding on a prosecution – a stipulation proposed by the Royal College of Physicians. Archbishop Peter Smith welcomed the revised guidelines; they showed, he said, that 'the law has not changed, that all cases will be investigated and that no one is being given immunity from prosecution under these guidelines.'

What the guidelines made clear was that the condition of the sufferer was not a relevant factor in the decision to prosecute. This was an important rejection of the assisted suicide lobby's arguments; a legal policy that assesses human worth on the basis of physical and mental ability would have sanctioned a new kind of segregation in our society, rendering the disabled and the terminally ill second-class citizens less deserving of the protection of the law. (In Oregon, for example, cancer patients have been offered assisted suicide as an alternative to treatment.) The guidelines therefore uphold vital principles in the law as it has long been framed, while making explicit what has long been understood – that extreme cases will not be prosecuted.

These concerns need addressing. There needs to be far better provision for the terminally ill than currently exists. Care provision has not kept pace with an ageing population. Advances in palliative care mean no one today need suffer extreme pain – yet not enough carers have been trained in how to administer palliative drugs.

Precisely because patients (on the whole) trust their doctors, legalisation is doubly dangerous: a doctor's willingness to supply the 'service' could easily be misread by a trusting patient as implying that it was the appropriate course of action to take in his or her condition. It is a terrible responsibility to lay on doctors – which is why most doctors are strongly opposed to a change in the law.

A call for palliative care

The Catholic view is that behind the drive to legalise assisted dying is the positive intention of seeking freedom from *unnecessary suffering* – the suffering associated with the indignity of dying in hospital, or the feeling of being a burden to others. These failures, which lie behind many of the calls to choose the time of dying, must be addressed – rather than accede to the calls for legalisation, which would reinforce those failures.

Consider the Netherlands and Belgium, where euthanasia is legal and palliative care provision far below UK standards. The architect of the 2001 Dutch euthanasia law, Els Borst, admitted in 2009 that the Government of the time was wrong to have introduced euthanasia without improving palliative care. Now that euthanasia has become socially acceptable in the Netherlands – in 2008 Dutch doctors reported 2,331 cases of euthanasia and 400 cases of assisted suicide – the pressure to improve palliative care has considerably lessened.

Some slopes really are slippery. In Oregon, the number of assisted suicide deaths has nearly quadrupled from 24 in 1998 to 95 in 2009, a figure which represents 19.3 per 10,000 deaths in the state. If a similar law were introduced in the UK, according to a report by the 'Living and Dying Well' think tank, more than 1,000 deaths by euthanasia or assisted suicide would occur each year. The experience of other countries also shows that the slope is slippery in other ways: what starts out as being intended for the terminally ill and those in extreme pain, gradually expands to include the elderly, the mentally ill and the merely depressed.

An assisted suicide law is unnecessary – advanced palliative care has transformed the relief of extreme pain. But it would also chill the environment for the dying, encouraging people to seek death as an alternative to the suffering they fear, or the burden they are worried they will be on others. A change in the law would meet the demands of a small number of highly determined people with strong convictions about personal autonomy; but it would put a far larger number of infirm and vulnerable people at risk. We need to increase the quality of people's end-of-life care, not evade the challenge through euthanasia.

Rather than defend the status quo, therefore, a Catholic Voice needs to be a passionate reformer – but in the direction of improving the quality of the journey at the end of life, not suicide. As the Archbishop of Westminster, Vincent Nichols, puts it: 'Even the most restricted of lives is lived in transcendence by virtue of being human. If we fail to see this and honour it, then we not only fail to respect a person: we do that person violence. There is a hidden violence in so many of our systems, even those of care, because their operational mode is reductionist. If we reduce death to a clinical event and manage it through a series of standard procedures then we do not deal with death well, either clinically or humanly.'

The existing frame

'A dignified death, free of pain at a moment of our own choosing is now possible. Why should the Church interfere with the choice of people who want to relieve their own suffering or those of their loved ones? Palliative care has made great steps forward but it is not always well applied and people are still kept alive unnecessarily in great pain. Some people want to be able to choose the moment of their own death themselves and the changing legislation clearly acknowledges public opinion on this matter. Why should it only be rich people, who can afford to go to Switzerland, who are allowed to choose the time of their death?'

Reframe

The reframing of this question involves making a passionate case for hospices and the spread of palliative care. Rather than condemn people to unnecessary suffering, we need to enhance the 'quality of death'. This is an area in which, because of the pioneering work of our hospices, the UK leads the way, according to the 'Quality of Death Index' devised by the Economist Intelligence Unit. The Index, which measures the environment for end-of-life care services across 40 countries, puts the UK top of the table, ranking first in the Quality of End of Life category, which includes indicators such as access to painkillers, availability of training, doctor – patient transparency, and so on. This is a record to be proud of, and it is one inextricably linked to the legal environment against euthanasia.

Key messages

Against changing the law

- The current law safeguards the vulnerable and upholds life – while showing compassion to those who break the law. Allowing assisted suicide would destroy the law's careful balance. The law would no longer defend the intrinsic value of every human life. The revised DPP prosecution guidelines ensure that the law does not imply that some lives are worth less than others

- Assisted suicide gives the green light to hopelessness and despair. It sanctions suicide as a response to hardship. It leaves the vulnerable more vulnerable – especially the disabled, whose lives may be judged less valuable in law. The right to die will become a duty to die.

- It will destroy the trust between doctor and patient.

- The drive to change the law comes from a small group of determined individuals who view life as something that can and should be under our absolute control. They are sincere in their beliefs; but what matters here is what is good for society. The law must uphold life and protect the vulnerable.

- As the experience of the Netherlands shows, euthanasia undermines palliative care.

In favour of extending palliative care

- A person who suffers is no less a person than one who doesn't. Some suffering in life will be unavoidable; it is part of the process of dying. But no one should nowadays endure unbearable pain.

- Britain is a world leader in hospices and palliative care. We need more, not fewer, of these. People suffering/in pain should be offered *real* choice – the choice not to suffer unnecessarily. Euthanasia does not solve that problem; it covers it up.

Chapter 5

Clerical sex abuse

Challenging questions

- *Why has it taken so long for the Church to take clerical sexual abuse seriously?*
- *Why were priests who had allegations of abuse against them routinely moved to other parishes where the abuse could continue?*
- *Why do bishops in some countries still blame the media rather than take the allegations seriously? And why aren't they reprimanded by Rome?*
- *What structures are in place to ensure that laicised priests don't simply disappear underground and continue to abuse children?*

Is the clerical sex abuse crisis, as some claim, the greatest threat to the Catholic Church since the Reformation? No. The mass executions of priests in the French and Mexican Revolutions and 1930s Spain, or the wholesale suppression and persecution of the Church in Stalinist Russia, presented a more pressing challenge to Catholic existence.

But crisis it certainly has been – not least for Catholics themselves, who have been shocked and saddened by an almost constant stream of revelations. As the Catholic bishops of England and Wales put it in April 2010, 'Catholics are members of a single universal body. These terrible crimes, and the inadequate response by some church leaders, grieve us all.' Media focus has been intense and incessant. The accusations – cover up of crimes, deafness to the voice of victims, sexual misconduct, abuse of trust – could hardly be worse. The conviction in newsrooms that the Church has been unaccountable, and needs to puts its house in order, has given the media a sense of moral entitlement in placing the Church under an unforgiving spotlight.

Without that spotlight, of course, the voice of the victims would not have been heard and vital reforms would never have happened – at least not as speedily. A Catholic Voice on this issue needs to begin by recognising that fact. The media's role has been, therefore, a positive one – although that does not excuse the distortions, exaggerations, myths, ignorance and lazy reporting, let alone the 'gotcha' relish, which has characterised many of the stories. 'What guided this press campaign was not only a sincere desire for truth,' said Pope Benedict in *Light of the World* (*LoW*), 'but there was also some pleasure in exposing the Church and if possible discrediting her.' But significantly he adds, 'we must be grateful for every disclosure'. The media has performed a necessary service.

In 2000–01, the Church in England and Wales – and especially the newly appointed Archbishop of Westminster, Cardinal Cormac Murphy-O'Connor – was subjected to a forensic examination by flagship BBC news programmes over the mishandling of paedophile priests. From January 2002, the crisis exploded in the United States, beginning in the archdiocese of Boston; for six months it was seldom off the front pages. In 2009, the focus was on Ireland, following two devastating reports (Ryan and Murphy); in 2010, it shifted to central Europe, and especially Germany. Mostly the scandals have concerned local churches; but the Vatican has been in the frame especially for its failure to deal quickly or adequately – especially in the last years of Pope John Paul II – with two notorious cases, that of the former Archbishop of Vienna, Cardinal Hans Gröer, and the founder of the Legionaries of Christ, Fr Marcial Maciel Degollado.

The scandal has had four principal elements:

1. *a moral crisis*: revelations that priests used their status to manipulate and coerce young people into illegal and immoral sexual relations;
2. *an institutional crisis*, in which the desire to preserve the Church's good name led to victims being silenced or paid off while the perpetrators went unpunished;
3. *a crisis of local church leadership*, as evidence emerges of bishops acting indulgently towards abusers and high-handedly towards victims – and above all, failing to reveal accusations to civil authorities;
4. *a crisis of universal church leadership*, centred on accusations that Rome failed to force local bishops to take action against abusive priests, or even obstructed that action, while failing to act against very senior figures such as Gröer and Maciel.

What has been ignored or under-reported by the news media are the countless ways in which the Church has sought to put its house in order through strict new guidelines and procedures, and tightening up on the internal church mechanisms to punish the perpetrators; all of which ensure that the crisis can never recur. Among the most important of these changes are:

1. Strict guidelines introduced by many – but not yet all – bishops' conferences across the world, which mandate immediate reporting of any accusation to the police and social services, and the immediate suspension of the accused priest. An example of early action was taken by the Church in England and Wales, which in 2001 set up a commission under Lord Nolan which led to guidelines and procedures which have made it a model institution, held up by the Government as an example for other institutions to follow. Soon after, the Dallas Norms introduced by the US bishops led to far-reaching reforms based on the 'zero tolerance' principle.

2. Vatican reforms beginning in 2001, which led to fast-track laicisation of abusive priests, the lifting of a statute of limitations to enable the punishment of abuse many decades ago, and the obligation to notify Rome of any substantial allegations of abuse, to ensure action is taken. In 2010 canon law was further updated to ensure speedy justice for victims, and a letter sent to all bishops' conferences urging the reporting of abuse cases to civil authorities;

3. Pope Benedict's letter to the Irish of 19 March 2010, possibly the most heartfelt apology ever offered by a Pope, which led to a Vatican-appointed delegation of cardinals to investigate dioceses and seminaries, and to put in place necessary reforms. The letter followed two devastating reports in 2009 which highlighted

chronic failures in the Irish bishops' handling of abuse claims over many decades; the reports led to the entire hierarchy being summoned to Rome, and the resignations of a number of bishops.

There are many more examples. A Vatican web page, 'Abuse of minors: the Church's response', is a useful compilation of actions and documents from Rome.

The overall picture, therefore, is one of serious flaws and failings being painfully exposed, leading to vigorous and far-reaching reforms. In Pope Benedict's words, it is 'a call to recognise again our fundamental values and to see the dangers that threaten not only priests but society as a whole' (*LoW*, #41). This catharsis is evident in a new attitude and a new resolve. Worldwide, much still remains to be done: having put in place reforms to ensure that the crisis can never recur, the Church's focus is now increasingly on the victims themselves, supporting them and helping them to heal, and placing the expertise and understanding gained at the service of wider society.

Positive intention

The positive intention behind the criticism of the Church couldn't be clearer: the protection of children from sexual abuse. The perception is that children were not and are not safe within the Church. The moral value behind the indignation is a deeply Christian one: the abuse of innocence, and the sacrifice of children on the altar of institutional reputation, are in clear violation of everything the Gospel stands for.

Putting the house in order

What causes anger and misunderstanding on this issue is the perception that Catholics 'just don't get it': they blame the victims or the media, or see the criticism as an excuse to bash the Church. Yet Catholics now, from Pope Benedict downwards, very much 'get it': even though the media played a key role in exposing the issue, it is the Church itself – Catholics in the pews, bishops, cardinals, the Vatican – which is bent on putting its house in order.

The crisis is not over, of course, until every bishops' conference across the globe ensures that allegations are never again brushed under the carpet. And there is still plenty of healing to do, together with compensation pay-outs. But across the western world – notably in the USA and the UK – reforms have been put in place by bishops which ensure that what happened in the 1960s – 80s cannot recur, reforms which make the Catholic Church in those countries a leader in safeguarding, to the point where the British Government, for example, recommends the UK Catholic Church procedures (see below) to other institutions as a model to follow. The Vatican has meanwhile drawn up global guidelines to ensure that the same will be said of the Church in other countries. Better screening of candidates to the priesthood, the punishment (in both civil and canon law) of perpetrators, review of historical files to ensure that if action was not taken then it is taken now, and efforts to assist and support victims – all these are part of the Church's new approach.

There is a central point which continually gets missed. This is a crisis about abuse which took place many decades ago which was *back then* mishandled. All the studies concur that clerical sexual abuse of minors increased steadily from the mid-1960s through to the late 1970s; it then declined in the 1980s, and remains low. Yet the opposite impression has been created by the fact that only in recent years have many of the victims (now in their thirties and forties) stepped forward, encouraged by therapists, lawyers or simply by the new awareness of and sympathy for victims of sexual abuse.

Back when the abuse happened, a different social mentality prevailed: the issue was never discussed; the press did not investigate; victims were silenced or stayed silent out of shame. The Church 'covered up' abuse; but so did society as a whole, especially institutions such as schools or orphanages. It is in families where most abuse took and continues to take place, and in families where silence has reigned most strongly.

In the same way, although there are exceptions – evidence of continued mishandling, for example, by some Irish dioceses – the Church in the West is now outstanding in reporting and making public any allegation, however historic, and sets an example for other institutions and society as a whole to follow. Again, because evidence of abuse decades ago continues to come to light now, the impression is created that the Church continues to mishandle abuse allegations, when the opposite is true.

Because of the intense focus on the Church's past mishandling, there is little attention given to the wider social problem of abuse and the absence of transparency in other institutions. In the UK, for example, there is no obligation on a school to make public an allegation of sex abuse against its staff, and no school ever does; no such allegations ever appear, for example, in Ofsted reports. There has been a massive silence on this issue, in which the institutions of society have been complicit.

Yet – and this point must be continually stressed – the fact that the Church has received massive, highly selective attention doesn't make it innocent. There is no excuse for its failures to hear the voice of the victim and to take a moral lead.

But equally, it is unfair to claim that Church-run institutions are hotbeds of abuse, or that the Catholic priesthood contains an exceptionally large number of abusers, or that the Church's 'cover-up' of allegations was uniquely pernicious. There is no credible evidence that Catholic clergy have abused young people at a rate different from the clergy of any other denomination, and much evidence that the rate is considerably lower than in secular professions which deal with children. But it is difficult to say exactly, because no other profession or Church has conducted a systematic survey in the way that the Catholic Church has. One of the few there have been – into schools – took place over seven months by the Associated Press in 2007. AP showed that sex abuse of children in US schools was widespread, and mostly unreported (or 'covered up'): it found '2,570 educators whose teaching credentials were revoked, denied, surrendered or sanctioned from 2001 through 2005 following allegations of sexual misconduct'. Professor Charol Shakescraft of Virginia University studied 290,000 cases of alleged abuse between 1991 and 2000; out of a sample of 225 teachers who admitted sexually abusing a pupil, not a single one had been reported to the authorities.

From the late 1980s, contemporary abuse allegations against Catholic priests sharply dropped. From the 1990s victims started to step forward in substantial numbers as a silent generation found its voice in lawsuits and news reports. Bishops put in place guidelines in the 1990s in the UK, Ireland, the US and elsewhere; but it was not until 2000–03, following a relentless series of media stories, that the Church really began to put its house in order. As a result of the 2003 reforms introduced by the bishops at Dallas, in 2009 there were just six contemporary allegations of abuse against US priests, in a Church of 65 million Catholics; in England and Wales, where Catholics number around 5 million, there were four allegations in 2007.

The most detailed report into the abuse in Catholic institutions was commissioned in 2002 by the US Catholic bishops from independent researchers, at a cost of $1.8 million. The highly regarded John Jay College of Criminal Justice in New York published the first part of its report, 'The Nature and Scope of the Problem of Sexual Abuse of Minors by Catholic Priests and Deacons in the United States', in 2004; the second part, 'The Causes and Context of Sexual Abuse of Minors by Catholic Priests in the United States, 1950–2010' came out in May 2011. The report examined all plausible allegations of abuse of minors by clergy in the period between 1950 and 2002. The researchers used a very low standard of proof for the charges – 'not withdrawn or known to be false' – rather than proof of guilt. Over that 50-year period, the study found, 4,392 out of around 100,000 clergy were accused – just over 4 per cent of all priests About 80 per cent of the accusations were of abuse alleged to have occurred between the 1960s and the 1980s; more than half of those accused were accused of a single incident. In total, there was an average of 200 accusations (not convictions) a year, although a closer examination of the statistics presents a more accurate picture. Just 149 individuals were responsible for a quarter of all abuse allegations. And 40 per cent of the allegations date from a six-year period in the late 1970s.

The second part of the report shows that by the mid-1980s, bishops knew that abuse was a problem, but they had no idea of its extent. 'Though more than 80% of cases now known had already occurred by 1985, only 6% of those cases had been reported to the dioceses by that time,' it says. The bishops did not know of the scale of the problem until the 1990s. The report also showed that, while abuse increased in the Church at the same time as it increased in wider society, it decreased in the Church from the 1980s (but not in wider society) because of the actions taken by the Church at the time.

The report does not exculpate church leaders, whose 'response typically focused on the priest-abusers rather than on the victims'. Bishops remained ignorant, too, of the effect of sexual abuse because they did not meet with victims before 2002; as knowledge of victim harm increased in society generally in the 1990s, so did the understanding by diocesan leaders. The failure of some bishops to take responsibility for the harms caused by priestly abuse was 'egregious in some cases', the report notes.

Among the report's other findings were these:

1. Although it is impossible to predict which men might abuse minors, certain factors – being abused as a child, stress, alcohol – contributed. Many priest abusers had difficulty in relating to adults.
2. Celibacy was not the cause of sexual abuse. The sexual abuse of minors by priests in the US 'increased steadily from the mid-1960s through the late 1970s, then declined in the 1980s and continued to remain low', the report notes; yet celibacy remained constant throughout this period.
3. Homosexuality was not the cause either. Although 81 per cent of the victims of clergy abuse were male, there are no data to indicate that homosexual orientation is a cause or risk factor for abuse of minors.
4. Poor seminary formation played a significant role in the crisis. Most offenders were ordained before the 1970s but did not generally abuse before then. Seminarians at the time had little or no exposure to a curriculum of what is now understood as 'human formation': the training in self-understanding and the development of emotional and psychological competence for a life of celibate chastity.

Noting that no other institution had undertaken a public study of sexual abuse, the John Jay report urged other organisations to follow suit. 'Only with such an understanding can effective prevention policies be articulated and implemented.'

In England and Wales over the past 40 years, less than half of 1 per cent of Catholic priests (0.4 per cent) have faced allegations of child abuse. Fewer have been found guilty.

The Catholic Church in the UK and the US is these days an exceptionally safe place for young people. But that does not mean that the Church has not failed, as Archbishop Vincent Nichols said in March 2010. Noting that 'one broken child is a tragedy and a disgrace; one case alone is enough to justify anger and outrage,' he said: 'Abuse damages, often irrevocably, a child's ability to trust another, to fashion stable relationships, to sustain self-esteem. When it is inflicted within a religious context, it damages that child's relationship to God. Today, not for the first time, I express my unreserved shame and sorrow for what has happened to many in the Church.' And he added: 'My shame is compounded, as is the anger of many, at the mistaken judgments made within the Church: that reassurance from a suspect could be believed; that credible allegations were deemed to be 'unbelievable'; that the reputation of the Church mattered more than safeguarding children. These wrong reactions arise whenever and wherever allegations of abuse are made, whether within a family or a Church. We have to insist that the safety of the child comes first because the child is powerless.'

Explaining the focus on the Church

If the Church has not been uniquely, or even especially, defective in dealing with abuse, why has it been singled out, scrutinised as no other institution has been? Much of the reporting reflects a prejudice in society about celibacy as 'unnatural', leading to the idea that celibate priests need a sexual 'escape valve'. Yet some 70 per cent of abuse of minors takes place within families, by married men. And there is no evidence that there is less abuse by married pastors in the Protestant or Anglican traditions. The 4 per cent figure identified by the John Jay study is consistent with male clergy from other traditions and significantly lower than the general male adult population (estimated to be around 8 per cent).

The main explanation for the intense focus on the Church lies in the way the cases first came to light. Because no other organisation has as many parishes, schools and orphanages, and because dioceses keep meticulous records that yield a reliable portrait of its personnel and abuse over the decades, the Church has been an obvious target for civil litigation. An individual accuses a priest of abuse; lawyers then use that case as a means of forcing a diocese to disclose its files on other abuse allegations, which then become the basis for a network of interlocking cases – and news stories. Most religious institutions are more decentralised, smaller, and therefore harder to analyse or prosecute – and few have assets on the scale of a Catholic diocese. That is one reason why it has been justifiable, economically and practically, for lawyers on behalf of claimants to bring civil claims against the Catholic Church rather than against other institutions.

In the 1990s a growing number of lawsuits were settled by dioceses through confidential settlements accompanied by confidentiality agreements. Because the priest perpetrators were frequently left unpunished, when these settlements later came to light, the media could easily portray them as proof that the Church was 'buying the victims' silence'. As lawyers began mounting more and more actions, a picture began to emerge of bishops failing to report abuse allegations and instead moving priests between parishes following those allegations; encountering an often dismissive and high-handed response, the media scented blood.

In 2000, an intense media scrutiny on Cardinal Cormac Murphy-O'Connor, then the Archbishop of Westminster, for failing to deal with a paedophile priest, Michael Hill, led the Cardinal to appoint a commission under Lord Nolan to look at how church procedures could be improved in England and Wales. A similar commission was created under Hussey in Ireland. These commissions would lead to sweeping reforms, at the heart of which was the immediate notification of police and social services whenever an allegation was received, and the suspension of the priest while the allegation was investigated.

In January 2002, the crisis exploded in the US after the *Boston Globe* persuaded judges to force the archdiocese of Boston to make public its confidential files. What emerged was a sorry picture of inaction, denial and confidential settlements that meant that the story was rarely off the front pages until June that year, when the US bishops in Dallas introduced far-reaching reforms – including the John Jay study mentioned above. In order to put a stop to the hugely damaging drip-drip of lawsuits, the bishops agreed to review their diocesan files to ensure that any allegation, however historic, would now be acted upon. In December 2002, Cardinal Bernard Law resigned.

Accounting for failure

How had these failures come about? There is no doubt that in a confined period (around the 1960s – 70s) substantial abuse took place within the priesthood – anywhere between 1,000 and 3,000 priests in the US sexually engaged with minors. Although this figure is consistent with rates of abuse by male clergy of other denominations, and considerably less than the male adult population in general, it is still a shocking number.

It's hard today to realise how little screening of candidates to the priesthood existed 30 years ago. As Dr Thomas Plante, professor of psychology at Santa Clara University, writes in his 2010 study, *A Perspective on Clergy Sexual Abuse*:

> 30 years ago, most priests entered seminary during high school, did not participate in a comprehensive psychological evaluation prior to admission, and had no training in sexuality, maintaining professional boundaries, and impulse control. Advice regarding dealing with sexual impulses included cold showers and prayer. Today, most applicants to the priesthood are much older (generally in their late 20s and 30s). They have often had satisfying and appropriate intimate relationships before entering the seminary. They have completed a psychological evaluation that specifically examines risk factors for sexual problems. They now get good training in sexuality and issues related to managing sexual impulses. It is not surprising that the majority of the

sex-offending priests that we hear about in the press are older. In fact, our research indicates that the average age of these men is 53.

The other dimension to the crisis was the failure by bishops to act on allegations and punish the perpetrators. Of course, as John Jay shows, bishops in the early 1980s had no idea of the scale of the problem. And the prevailing psychiatric wisdom of the time was that paedophilia was an illness that could be managed or controlled with medication and therapy. Yet the reluctance of bishops to punish sexually abusive priests was still remarkable. A common myth is that bishops resorted to canon law rather than civil law in dealing with abusive priests, and that canon law had no real sanctions. In fact, canon law demands that a bishop investigate an allegation of sexual abuse and, if true, expel the abuser from the priesthood – something that should occur parallel to, not instead of, prosecution by police.

Yet neither happened. The application of the penalties in the Church's own law had fallen into disuse. After the mid-1960s in Ireland, notes Pope Benedict in *Light of the World*, ecclesiastical penal law 'was simply not applied any more. The prevailing mentality was that the Church must not be a Church of laws, but rather, a Church of love; she must not punish. Thus the awareness that punishment can be an act of love ceased to exist. This led to an odd darkening of the mind, even in very good people.'

The Murphy Commission report into the diocese of Dublin's mishandling of abuse allegations from the 1960s to the 1980s found that none of its four archbishops ever reported the abuse that was brought to their attention, and no canonical trials ever took place. The report documents a 'collapse of respect for canon law … Offenders were neither prosecuted nor made accountable within the Church.' The normal response was for a bishop to send an abusive priest for therapy, in line with the thinking of the time – that paedophilia was a kind of psychological illness that could be cured. Later, it would be seen as a 'fixation' or 'orientation' that resisted therapy. The problem, however, was not with the use of therapy per se, but the way it was used as an alternative to punishing acts criminal in both civil and canon law.

In his *Pastoral Letter to the Catholics of Ireland* of 19 March 2010, Pope Benedict XVI addresses this specific failure of the bishops.

> It cannot be denied that some of you and your predecessors failed, at times grievously, to apply the long-established norms of canon law to the crime of child abuse. Serious mistakes were made in responding to the allegations. I recognise how difficult it was to grasp the extent and complexity of the problem, to obtain reliable information and to make the right decisions in the light of conflicting expert advice. Nevertheless, it must be admitted that grave errors of judgement were made and failures of leadership occurred. All this has seriously undermined your credibility and effectiveness.

However, there were also obstacles in Rome to the most extreme punishment in canon law – the laicisation of priests. One of the reasons that bishops around the world typically did not try to laicise abusive priests during the 1980s and 1990s was because the legal procedures for doing so were perceived as lengthy, cumbersome and uncertain. Although it falls to the local bishop to act against an abusive priest – by suspending him, reporting him to the authorities, and so on – the procedure for laicising him is reserved to Rome. Petitions for dispensation from the obligations of priesthood were handled by the Congregation for the Doctrine of the Faith (CDF), headed by Cardinal Ratzinger from 1980 until 2005. An indication of the frustration he felt at being unable swiftly to dismiss abusive priests came to light recently in the form of a 1998 letter which he wrote to another cardinal, José Rosalío Castillo Lara, calling for a more rapid and simplified penal process.

He did not prevail on that occasion, but did succeed in persuading Pope John Paul II to give the CDF greater responsibility for dealing with such cases. Later, in a 2001 *motu propio* (a change to the law on the Pope's personal initiative) of John Paul II called *Sacramentorum Sanctitatis Tutela*, two vital reforms were introduced: bishops were made to forward to the CDF all credible cases of abusive priests, to ensure action was taken; secondly, the laicisation process was fast-tracked so that abusive priests could be laicised by means of decree rather than a church court trial. The reforms were further tightened in 2003 and 2010.

Prior to those reforms, the laicisation of abusive priests took too long, as three cases from the 1970s which came to light in the US in the course of 2010 showed. Murphy in Wisconsin, Teta in Arizona, and Kiesle in California had in common a number of facts:

the abuse took place in the 1970s; the police were informed and acted; the priest was suspended by his bishop; requests for dismissal from the clerical state ('laicisation') were sent to Cardinal Ratzinger's department in the Vatican, the Congregation for the Doctrine of the Faith; delays of many years then followed; eventually the priests were defrocked – except in the case of Murphy, who died during his trial.

Yet it is not true that these delays somehow enabled the priests in each case to continue abusing. Suspension and laicisation are two separate actions. The first can be done by a bishop, with immediate effect; the second is a lengthy process that involves Rome. Suspension – meaning a priest is no longer able to function as a priest: say Mass, hear confession, act as chaplain etc – is the key action that a bishop has to take against an abusive priest to prevent him having contact with minors. If, in any of these 'smoking gun' cases, the bishop failed to suspend an abusive priest immediately, he did wrong. But these failures cannot be pinned on Rome, which before the reforms of 2001 only came into the picture when a request for laicisation landed on the desk of the CDF. Before 2001 it failed to act swiftly in processing those requests. This was tragic for the victim who saw that his abuser remained in the priesthood. And it was put right with the 2001 reforms. But even before then there is no evidence that delays in laicisation enabled or encouraged priests to continue abusing.

Canon law, civil law

The changes introduced by Cardinal Ratzinger in 2001 mean that nowadays clergy convicted (in civil courts) of the sexual abuse of minors – or where the evidence of that abuse is overwhelming – are swiftly expelled from the priesthood by means of an 'ex officio' dismissal signed by the Pope, without any need for a lengthy church trial . But even in cases where the police have dropped charges (for lack of evidence, say), the Church still proceeds with its own investigation and trials. After reviewing the evidence, the CDF might authorise the local bishop to conduct either a full penal trial (before a local church tribunal) or an 'administrative penal process', which does not involve a trial. If the priest is judged guilty, canonical penalties may be imposed, including laicisation.

Note that these canonical processes occur alongside – in fact, almost always after – the investigation, trial and conviction of the abusive priest by the police and courts of that country. Civil and canon penalties are not alternatives. They exist in two parallel spheres; each has jurisdiction the other lacks. For example, civil law is capable of punishing by imprisoning; church law is not; but church law can laicise a priest, which is not something civil law can do. A possible analogy – one easily understood in the professional world – is that of associations or clubs with their own internal regulations. A barrister who commits fraud will be investigated by police and, if guilty, sentenced to a term in prison. But he will also be subject to punishment by the Bar Council, which will withdraw his membership. These are separate jurisdictions: the Bar Council cannot imprison the offender; the civil courts cannot strike him off the Bar Council list of bona fide barristers. Each jurisdiction has its own sanctions.

Action or inaction in one jurisdiction does not prevent action or inaction in the other. The Bar Council might decide to expel a member for conduct which brings the legal profession into disrepute, even when this conduct has not involved breaking any law or when the police have decided not to pursue the matter. In the same way, the Church will often choose to pursue an allegation when the civil authorities have not. And even when the police have dropped charges against a priest, the accused priest must still go through a rigorous process of 'risk assessment' by Church-appointed experts before he is allowed back into his parish.

Why does the Vatican not instruct bishops across the world to report any allegation they receive to the civil authorities? Firstly, there is no need: the assumption of canon law is always that civil law be obeyed. As the Vatican's guidelines for understanding CDF procedures make clear: 'Civil law concerning reporting of crimes to the appropriate authorities should always be followed.' But faced with evidence that bishops in different parts of the world have been less than keen to divulge cases to the police and social services, why does the Vatican not mandate that they do so? Rome does, indeed, 'encourage' reporting every accusation to civil authorities. But *mandating* such reporting would be impossible, given the wide variety of legal circumstances in which the Church operates. But at the time of writing, Rome has asked every bishops' conference which has not done so to draw up rules for dealing with abusive priests, and these should be in place in 2012.

There are many myths about the 2001 document issued by Cardinal Ratzinger. It has often been claimed that it 'ordered a cover-up' by insisting that parties to an abuse allegation observe secrecy under pain of excommunication. *De Delictis Gravioribus* (2001) updated an earlier (1962) canonical document, *Crimen Sollicitationis*, which lawyers in the US bringing claims on behalf of abuse victims have tried to use as evidence of a 'cover-up' of abuse ordered by the Vatican. This kite-flier passed seamlessly into a BBC *Panorama* TV programme, 'Sex crimes and the Vatican', broadcast in October 2006, and has become an enduring myth.

Yet the document was concerned with a specifically canonical crime, namely the use of the confessional to solicit sexual favours. It imposes strict confidentiality during the trial and investigation precisely to allow the victims to give evidence freely and to protect the accused until found guilty – in other words, to ensure action is taken. These regulations are entirely within the jurisdiction of canon law. There is nothing in that document preventing victims reporting the case to their local police – and the assumption is that they would.

Ignorance of canon law, or the misreading of it to try to claim that the Church had a systematic policy of obstructing civil law, is at the origin of many of the false accusations against the Church in general, and Pope Benedict in particular, over clerical sex abuse. Neither Church nor media are innocent in this. The Church needs to do a much better job of explaining what canon law is and the media needs to do a better job of researching before uncritically reproducing wild allegations.

It is very easy for these misunderstandings quickly to harden into misleading news stories. When, in June 2010, Pope Benedict issued updates to the canon law on 'serious crimes', the *Normae de Gravioribus Delictis*, it was reported that he had caused offence to Anglicans and women by putting the attempted ordination of women on a par with the sexual abuse of children. The Norms extended the statute of limitations still further, allowing abuse victims to bring accusations more than 20 years after their eighteenth birthday, made the offence of possession or distribution of child pornography equal to that of abuse of minors, and made other changes to ensure swifter justice for victims and abusive priests. Because the Norms dealt with abuses of the sacraments – namely Holy Orders – the document also included other penalties, such as those imposed on a bishop who tried to ordain a woman. But the fact that these penalties fell into the same section of canon law did not imply they were morally equivalent.

Rome takes charge

Until the year 2000, the clerical sex abuse crisis was confined to the local Church – a question that needed to be tackled by bishops, rather than by the Vatican. But a few high-profile, damaging cases put the spotlight on Rome. Although Pope John Paul II met American cardinals in 2002 to discuss the US clerical sex abuse crisis, before his death in 2005 there was a tendency for cardinals in Rome to blame the media, or to see abuse as an 'Anglo-Saxon' problem. The great exception was Cardinal Ratzinger, who unsuccessfully sought to persuade Pope John Paul II to take action in two cases – those of Gröer and Maciel.

Cardinal Hans Hermann Gröer, Archbishop of Vienna from 1986 to 1995, was forced to step down after various former students and monks stepped forward to accuse him of molesting them. Austria's statute of limitations meant he could not be prosecuted. In 1998 Cardinal Ratzinger sought to persuade Pope John Paul II to investigate, but this was blocked by the then Secretary of State, Cardinal Sodano. As a result, although he was suspended as an abbot, Cardinal Gröer was never laicised before his death.

An even more notorious case was that of Fr Marcial Maciel Degollado, the Mexican founder of an order of more than 600 priests, the Legionaries of Christ, and its lay arm, Regnum Christi. From 1956 to his death he led a double life, constantly engaged in financial and sexual misconduct and drug abuse, maintaining relationships with at least two women and fathering six children, two of whom he abused. Former members had made accusations of sexually abusive acts by Maciel since the 1980s. Finally, in 2001, the Congregation for Doctrine of the Faith began to investigate. In 2005, after Pope Benedict's election, his successor at the CDF, Cardinal William Levada, suspended Maciel, then 84, from ministry; he was ordered to live a life of prayer and penitence. A canonical trial was ruled out because of his advanced age (he died two years later).

In 2009, the Vatican appointed a panel of five bishops to investigate the order. In March 2010, the Legionaries admitted that their founder had been guilty of abuse and illicit relationships, and apologised. Maciel was formally denounced by the Vatican in 2010 for creating a 'system of power' built on silence and obedience that enabled him to lead an 'immoral' double life 'devoid of scruples and authentic religious sentiment', which allowed him to abuse boys unchecked over many decades. The Vatican also acknowledged the 'hardships' faced by Maciel's accusers over many years when they were ostracised or ridiculed, and commended their 'courage and perseverance to demand the truth'.

According to John Allen, the veteran Vatican-watcher, the then-Cardinal Joseph Ratzinger underwent 'a sort of conversion experience' around 2001, when the sex abuse crisis landed in his lap following Pope John Paul II's *Motu Propio*. The case files he reviewed opened his eyes. 'The story as I know it', wrote Allen, 'boils down to this: before 2001, Ratzinger was essentially another cardinal in denial; afterwards, he became the leading force inside the Vatican for a more aggressive response.'

Since his election as Pope in 2005, Benedict XVI has moved decisively on the issue – introducing reforms, clearing Vatican logjams, issuing statements, and on his foreign trips meeting abuse victims. The massive increase in activity from the Vatican on this issue can be seen on the Vatican web page dedicated to documenting the Church's response to abuse. Among the pontifical documents are more than a dozen by Benedict XVI, compared with two by Pope John Paul II.

Summarising the Pope's record on this issue, Gregory Erlandson and Matthew Bunson write in *Pope Benedict XVI and the Sexual Abuse Crisis*:

> From leading the CDF's efforts before and after 2001 in reviewing the case files of suspect priests to his own efforts to address the issue forthrightly as pope, Benedict has grown into a leadership role on this issue just when the Church most needed him. He has met with victims. He has rebuked

the abuser priests. He has challenged the bishops. He has overseen a series of procedural reforms that have allowed the Church to respond more quickly when it is necessary to restrict, suspend or even laicise a priest.

Safeguarding in the UK: an example praised by the Pope

During his UK visit Pope Benedict spoke passionately about 'the immense suffering caused by the abuse of children, especially within the Church and by her ministers' at a Mass he celebrated at Westminster Cathedral. Expressing his deep sorrow 'to the innocent victims of these unspeakable crimes', he spoke of 'the shame and the humiliation which all of us have suffered because of these sins'. Later he met abuse victims, and assured them that 'the Catholic Church is continuing to implement effective measures designed to safeguard young people, and that it is doing all in its power to investigate allegations, to collaborate with civil authorities and to bring to justice clergy and religious accused of these egregious crimes.'

He also that day met, for the first time on any of his visits, a group of safeguarding professionals and volunteers in the Catholic Church, praising them for ensuring that 'the preventative measures put in place are effective, that they are maintained with vigilance, and that any allegations of abuse are dealt with swiftly and justly'.

The then chairman of the National Catholic Safeguarding Commission of England and Wales, Bill Kilgallon, said the Pope had been impressed by the fact that 'there was one set of policies and procedures for the whole Church, for the dioceses and the religious orders, that they all subscribe to', that independent oversight was built into the procedures at every level, and that civil authorities (police and social services) are alerted as soon as an allegation is made. Later, Kilgallon explained the system as he had explained it to Pope Benedict:

1. Each parish has a representative – a volunteer, a lay person – who takes responsibility for implementing safeguarding practice in the parish.
2. Within each diocese, there is a Safeguarding Officer – sometimes more than one – who is usually professionally qualified. Each diocese has a Safeguarding Commission made up of people drawn from relevant professions such as the police, the probation services, social services, health and the law. The Commission has an Independent Chair. Religious Orders have similar structures.
3. Nationally, the Church has the National Catholic Safeguarding Commission (NCSC), whose task is to set the safeguarding policies of the Church and to monitor compliance. The Catholic Safeguarding Advisory Service (CSAS) is the Church's national office staffed with experts in safeguarding, training and development.
4. In England and Wales, the policies and procedures apply to the whole Church: not just to the dioceses, but also to religious orders. The NCSC is mandated by the Conference of Bishops and the Conference of Religious.

5. All allegations are reported either to the police or social services, or both, depending on the nature of the allegations. 'We work in co-operation with the statutory authorities throughout the procedure – this brings a clear element of independence into the whole process.'
6. Anybody working in the Church, whether in full-time ministry or as volunteers, are strictly vetted before they work with children and with vulnerable adults.

The existing frame

'The Catholic Church, both locally and in Rome, ignored and covered up the sexual abuse of children by priests for decades and continues to do so. It sought to silence the victims and refused to take action. Pope Benedict is particularly culpable in the cover-up. Celibate priests are more likely to abuse children than others. The Church is an organisation that continues to be hostile to media revelations and is still a dangerous place for children.'

Reframe

The appalling crime of the clerical sex abuse of minors is a profound betrayal of priests' calling and the Gospel. For many years, the Church, like other institutions, failed to grasp the extent of sexual abuse and its compulsive nature; decades ago, it mishandled accusations and failed to punish the perpetrators. But in the past ten years, it has gone further than any other institution in putting in place vital reforms to ensure it can never happen again. Those reforms have made the Church transparent, accountable, and one of the safest places for young people. From 2001, when John Paul II gave him responsibility for dealing with sex abuse cases, Cardinal Ratzinger/Pope Benedict has led the reforms from the Vatican to ensure that across the world the Church never again covers up and fails to hear the voice of the victims. The apologies from church leaders – the Pope, cardinals, bishops – have been forthright and thorough, and most importantly, they have taken action. In the UK the system of safeguarding is exceptional, and recommended as a model for other institutions to follow. Increasingly, that can also be said of the Church in other countries too.

Key messages

- *Moral awakening.* Society and its institutions have woken up to the prevalence of the sexual abuse of minors. Like other institutions 30–40 years ago, Catholic schools and parishes did not act on allegations and the victims were not heard. There has been a sea change in the Church's attitudes and policies.
- *Media has helped the Church to change.* The media's job is to probe and to hold to account, and they have shone a light on some dark corners in the Church, which has spurred the Church to change its attitudes and procedures. Many of the reports have been hysterical and misleading. But we don't resent or reject the media holding us to account; we want to help them get their facts right.
- *Priesthood is not a haven for abusers.* The Catholic priesthood is not, nor has it ever been, exceptional in the number of abusers in its ranks. There is no causal

link between priestly celibacy and clerical sex abuse. The Church is now much more careful about who it accepts to the priesthood.

- *UK/US Church is a safe environment for young people.* The system of safeguarding is exceptional, and recommended as a model for other institutions to follow. Independent oversight is built in at every stage, and all allegations, however old, are automatically referred to police and social services.
- *No conflict between canon and civil law.* One isn't above or below the other. Put simply, all Catholics must obey the law – that's what canon law itself calls for. Both civil law and canon law regard the sexual abuse of minors as an extremely serious crime. The big difference between now and 30 years ago is that the Church acts on both laws – reporting allegations to the police *and* to the Vatican.
- *Pope Benedict has taken the lead in reforming the Vatican's approach.* Both as Cardinal and as Pope he has spearheaded vigorous reforms, acting decisively to combat what has been sometimes a culture of denial. He has made vital changes to church law to ensure perpetrators are swiftly punished.

Chapter 6

Catholic schools

Challenging questions
- *Why should schools which restrict admissions on the basis of faith receive public funds?*
- *Don't faith schools encourage intolerance and segregation?*
- *Doesn't the religious practice stipulation effectively bias admissions in favour of the middle classes – introducing social selection behind the screen of religious selection?*

Faith schools are a battleground of the wider neuralgic debate over equality versus religious freedom because – unlike other European countries – the British state funds faith schools. About one in three state-funded primary schools, and around one in five secondary schools, are schools of a religious character.

Almost two-thirds of the faith secondary schools are Catholic. They are of a high standard and are popular, with a strong ethos rooted in local church institutions (parishes, religious orders, dioceses) and the teachings of the Church. For Catholics, their schools are testament to the strengths and values of their faith and their community. That shared ethos creates – Catholics would want to add: by means of Grace, through the Eucharist – strong personal relationships of trust which are behind the family spirit often commented on in Catholic schools. Preserving that ethos means, evidently, selecting to leadership positions in schools men and women who witness to their Catholic beliefs in their lives, and by admitting predominantly those children of practising Catholics.

These admissions criteria, which critics deplore as 'discrimination', have made Catholic, along with other faith schools, the target of secularists. Critics say faith schools embody and perpetuate sectarianism, reinforce social divisions and indoctrinate young people.

Some secularists believe that atheism should be taught as scientifically true; others (humanists, for example) call for secular or agnostic schools in which faith is not taught as true but as matter for relative study. All agree that faith should be excluded altogether from the schools' criteria for employment and admission, something which, as they are well aware, would have the effect of destroying the much-vaunted 'Catholic ethos'. Because of the practical and political impossibility of 'banning' faith schools, therefore, their critics call for them to be, in effect, secularised and neutered.

But as long as church schools remain popular, with a capacity for mobilising support – a few years ago, the Labour Government backed down from imposing quotas of non-faith children after MPs were flooded with protests – there seems little risk of this ambition succeeding. Many leaders in society are sympathetic to the secularist arguments, however, and think of faith schools as inimical to social ideals of equality. The continued existence of state-maintained faith schools cannot, therefore, be taken for granted, and Catholic Voices need to know how to combat the arguments against them and to understand the case for them.

Behind the secularist critique is a basically individualist and statist view of education, one which, ever since the French Revolution, has seen schools as the places where states can engineer citizens. In this view, the social divisions in society should gradually be overcome by creating schools in which religious and other differences are left at the school gate – or at least, placed into a neutral melting-pot in which the only truth is that of rational, technocratic, secular creeds.

For the Church, however, schools are delegates of the family and parish, not projections of the state. The state should regulate, encourage and support, but it is civil society, not the state, which organises the teaching of children. The idea that children should be formed in the image of the state is a deeply authoritarian concept.

Put positively, schools at their best reflect the vigour of civil society – the strong values of religious and other institutions – rather than the state. That doesn't mean, obviously, that only Churches should run schools; but it does mean that, in so far as they can, *communities* should. Education is at its best the closer it is to communities – a core principle of the social Catholic doctrine of subsidiarity. And because, in the Church's view, education is not a merely utilitarian matter – it is about formation in habits and virtues as well as academic development – it cannot exclude the transcendent, religious dimension. 'It is about forming the human person, equipping him or her to live life to the full – in short, it is about imparting wisdom,' said Pope Benedict XVI on his visit to the UK, addressing educators at St Mary's College, Twickenham. 'And true wisdom is inseparable from knowledge of the Creator.'

As a result of the French and successive revolutions, in many European countries the state took over teaching from the Church, leaving the Church to run private schools. But in the UK, the Church has continued to own and run schools – even while they are funded by the taxpayer. Under an agreement between Church and state in 1944 (see below), Catholic schools became voluntary-aided, that is, part of the state system of education, but retaining the freedom to run themselves according to their principles. As a result, state secondary education in the UK today is a mixture of community (non-religious) schools and faith schools, either voluntary-aided or voluntary-controlled. Some Catholic schools are also set to become 'academy' schools.

In England, about a third of primary and just below 20 per cent of secondary schools are of a religious character, mostly Anglican and Catholic, but including other Christian denominations, as well as Jewish, Muslim and Sikh schools. Of the 16,971 state-maintained primary schools, just over 6,000 are faith schools: 4,409 Church of England, 1,693 Catholic. Of the 3,333 state-funded secondary schools, 207 are Church of England and 344 are Catholic.

There are close to 2,300 Catholic schools in England and Wales, about 10 per cent of the total number. Almost all are voluntary-aided (maintained); some 150 are independent schools. There are also three Catholic academies and 2,021 schools run jointly with other Churches, as well as three higher education institutions (St Mary's, Twickenham; Leeds Trinity; Newman College, Birmingham) plus Liverpool Hope University, which is a joint Catholic – Anglican university college. In total, Catholic schools and colleges educate nearly 800,000 students.

Positive intention

The criticism of Catholic schools – and faith schools in general – rests on an Enlightenment ideal of equality and a suspicion of religion as divisive. Because the positive intention of the secularist-humanist criticism is compelling – education should foster tolerance and free thinking, not harden social divisions – it is all too easy for Catholic Voices to be 'heard' arguing against those values, for the 'right to discriminate' or the 'right to bring up our children as we see fit'. Such language and arguments reinforce the idea of Catholics as separate and segregationist, promoting values at odds with modern liberal democracies. The widespread fear of Islamic extremism, associated with 'closed' mosque cultures, can but affect the way faith and faith schools in particular are seen.

Catholic schools: a brief history

The Catholic Church was the first provider of schools and universities in England. 'The transcendent dimension of study and teaching was clearly grasped by the monks who contributed so much to the evangelisation of these islands,' Pope Benedict told teachers at St Mary's, Twickenham, in September 2010. 'I am thinking of the

Benedictines who accompanied St Augustine on his mission to England, of the disciples of St Columba who spread the faith across Scotland and Northern England, of St David and his companions in Wales.'

Monasteries had libraries and schools. 'It was the monks' dedication to learning as the path on which to encounter the incarnate Word of God', Benedict XVI added, 'that was to lay the foundations of our western culture and civilization.'

Between the Reformation and 1850, when the Catholic Bishops of England and Wales were once again able publicly to practise their faith and establish schools, Catholic education went underground or abroad, but never ceased.

After 1850, schools sprung up to educate the children of the burgeoning Irish immigrant populations, often run by missionary religious orders. Because of the importance of education to the formation and development of the whole person, Catholic schools were often built before churches; the congregation would gather in the schoolrooms for Mass. These are schools, therefore, *born from* the community, *serving* the community, and often acting as the lynchpin of the relationships in that community.

The Church educated the poor long before the state stepped in. Serving the most disadvantaged and underprivileged has always been central to the mission of Catholic education – as it is today, when Catholic schools are vital to newly arrived immigrant families from Eastern Europe, Africa, Asia and Latin America. Catholic schools are the most ethnically diverse and international of all maintained schools in England and Wales.

In 1944 the education landscape in England and Wales was transformed by the Butler Act which promised to provide secondary education to all and increased the school leaving age to 15. As a result of the Act, the Church became responsible for the education of all baptised Catholic children, whatever the commitment of their parents to the Church and its teaching. It was an unusual, and remarkable, example of state – Church collaboration, and a recognition by the British Government that Catholic schools serve the common good.

Under the Butler Act Catholic schools mostly became voluntary-aided. They became part of the state system, but retained their own management and ownership. The funding was shared between the foundations which owned the schools – usually dioceses or religious orders – and the state. Today, the Church contributes around £20 million a year towards the capital cost of its schools.

Excellence

Ofsted inspection data from 2005 to 2009 shows that teaching and learning, the curriculum and other activities, as well as the quality of care, guidance and support, are all more likely to be better in faith schools than other schools. On the last criterion Catholic secondary schools did particularly well, 45 per cent showing outstanding care for their pupils, compared to 33 per cent of all schools. In its assessment of the overall personal development and well-being of learners, far more Catholic sixth forms were outstanding – 57 per cent compared to 40 per cent of all schools – than the average. Ofsted inspections consistently rate Catholic schools higher than average across all inspection criteria. For example:

- Ofsted inspections of schools' overall effectiveness show that higher proportions of Catholic schools and colleges are placed in the 'good' and 'outstanding' categories. Ofsted inspections in 2008/2009 judged eight out of ten Catholic primary schools to have achieved this standard compared with seven out of ten schools nationally. Similarly, eight out of ten Catholic secondary schools were judged to be outstanding or good compared with six out of ten schools nationally.
- Following Ofsted inspections (between September 2005 and July 2009) into how well learners achieved in schools in England, the same pattern emerged: the Catholic sector had an 8 per cent advantage in the primary phase and 11 per cent in the secondary phase. Catholic schools came out particularly well in the assessment of the standards reached and progress made by learners across the whole ability range, including those with learning difficulties.
- The same inspections showed far more Catholic schools gaining the highest rating for learners' personal development and well-being.
- In 2009 Ofsted rated just over half of all Catholic schools as 'outstanding', 'excellent' or 'very good' with regard to students' spiritual, moral, social and cultural development – far higher than the average of under 40 per cent of national schools. This category of inspection measures factors such as learners' attitudes to bullying, effective discussion in lessons, and readiness to engage with others from a different cultural background.

Responding to Accord

Accord, a lobby campaigning for religious organisations to be deprived of their exemptions from equality legislation, argues that 'in a pluralist, multi-cultural society, the state should promote tolerance and recognition of different values and beliefs'. No one could argue with that: a multicultural, multi-faith society cannot afford bigotry and intolerance.

Accord adds: 'Given the dangers of segregation and the importance of community cohesion we need schools that welcome all and are committed to non-discrimination. Schools should promote a culture of questioning, of knowledge, of respect and of exploration of values, where students develop their own identities and sense of place in the world.' Again, these would be values Catholic schools would be happy to subscribe to.

But Accord goes on to argue for five changes which would have the effect of undermining, not promoting, those values: admissions policies which take no account of pupils' religion or beliefs; recruitment and employment policies which do not discriminate on the grounds of religion or belief; 'an objective, fair and balanced syllabus for education about religious and non-religious beliefs'; and 'inclusive, inspiring and stimulating assemblies in place of compulsory acts of worship'. Accord also believes faith schools should have a single inspection regime for religious education, citizenship and PSHE (Personal, Social and Health Education).

Although Accord is supported by some religious groups, its secularist agenda is clear: to remove the distinctive faith element from schools in the name of encouraging equality and tolerance. Removing the right of Catholic schools to pick pupils predominantly from Catholic families and recruit Catholic staff to key posts would result, over time, in an end to that ethos. If that were ever achieved – if Catholic schools, in other words, ceased being Catholic – would they be better at promoting community cohesion, tolerance, intellectual openness, and a strong sense of students' identity and their place in the world?

The evidence all points the other way. Catholic schools are regularly applauded by independent inspectors for being better than other (mostly non-religious) schools in these areas.

Catholic Voices need gently to point to this evidence, and point out that the educational outcomes which Accord and other secularist-humanist critics want to see are precisely those which Catholic schools already impart – more successfully than other schools. (This is something which they fail to see because of their dogmatic conviction that religion narrows the mind and divides people off from each other.) Furthermore, these positive aims are crucial not just to the Catholic ethos of education but Catholic teaching and values more generally, embodied in Catholic Social Teaching.

Diversity and tolerance

Since 2007, maintained schools in England have a duty to promote 'community cohesion', meaning (a) respect for diversity by seeking to understand others; (b) equality of opportunity to enable young people to attain their full potential; (c) participation in and engagement with the wider community. The term also means building a 'cohesive community', by which is meant a common vision and sense of belonging, the appreciation of those of different backgrounds and circumstances, and encouraging strong and positive relationships between people within schools and neighbourhoods. To these were later added solidarity and community action, social justice, sense of rights and responsibilities, contribution of communities to a shared vision, and a sense of trust in institutions – all areas in which Catholic schools already excelled.

Pupils at Catholic schools are more likely to be from ethnic minority backgrounds than other schools: 27 per cent compared with 22.5 per cent in other schools. In terms of numbers of pupils in care or receiving free school meals, the proportion of pupils in Catholic maintained schools is average. Yet Catholic schools permanently exclude fewer pupils (0.09 per cent) than other schools (0.11 per cent) in England and Wales.

As part of a global Church – the largest transnational civil society organisation in the world – Catholics are quite used to living with, and celebrating, racial and social differences. Because of their links to parishes and charities, and their identification with the community, Catholic schools show outstanding examples of relationships of trust. A strong sense of solidarity, and a clear narrative of working with others of different or no faith for the common good of society, are key to Catholic social teaching. The Catholic approach is essentially relational or personal: people are conceived primarily not as isolated individuals but as 'a community of mutually dependent persons', in the words of the Archbishop of Westminster, Vincent Nichols.

A 2009 University of York study of the results of Ofsted inspections of community cohesion in schools concluded that faith schools are outstanding in this respect. The data surveyed, said Professor David Jenson, 'provides a useful corrective to some misguided assumptions about the roles that faith schools play within their communities' – namely the myth that faith schools close people off from wider society rather than help them to engage with and serve society. The evidence produced by independent inspection regimes, he said, 'entirely discredits those opinions'.

And it does. Catholic schools in England and Wales are more diverse in their social and racial composition, and score more highly in inspections of community cohesion, than other schools nationally. Ofsted inspection data analysed between September 2005 and July 2009 show that, for example, 41 per cent of Catholic secondary schools made an outstanding contribution to their communities, as opposed to 24 per cent of all schools. That means that Catholic schools are almost twice as likely as other schools to contribute to the building up of their local community.

As a 2008 Catholic Education Service report (*Catholic schools and community cohesion: CES guidance*) points out, 'for the Catholic community there is nothing optional about striving for a cohesive society. The Second Vatican Council urged Catholics to read the signs of the times and to engage with the world around them.'

That report cites countless examples of schools helping to build communities caring for the vulnerable, often through the local parish or Catholic charitable outreach project; putting pressure on local businesses to pay a living wage; creating safe streets by building links between schools and shops; raising money for developing countries; offering credit unions and adult education; fostering links with other schools where pupils are of a different faith, and creating projects aimed at them understanding each other's beliefs; enabling recycling locally – the list is almost endless.

Concern, respect, hospitality are also values which Catholic schools work to instil. For the average 30 per cent of pupils who are not Catholics, the schools make special provision at key religious times and seasons, while ensuring they are fully included in the life of the school. Catholic schools also collaborate with other schools and faith traditions and those of no religious character, contributing to the life of the local community in countless ways.

Admission, selection

As we saw in Chapter 3, faith schools have been exempted from some aspects of equality legislation in order to preserve their freedom to be what they are – their ethos. The law recognises that, just as it is not discriminatory to refuse to employ a committed carnivore as the director of a vegetarian charity, nor is it discriminatory to refuse to employ as principal of a Catholic school one whose belief or lifestyle is incompatible with the values the school embodies. When it comes to employing people, therefore, the Catholic school has – and needs to continue to have – the same freedom to select people from a pool of those in sympathy with its ethos as do other charities and civil-society actors. But staff in Catholic schools are very far from all being Catholic. In fact only three-fifths of teachers in maintained schools and colleges are Catholic – about 70 per cent in primary schools, less than 50 per cent in secondary schools.

Catholic schools were created primarily to serve the Catholic community, and that remains their principal role. They are allowed, therefore, to select the majority of their students from practising Catholic families. But not all: government guidelines tell faith schools to admit at least 15 per cent of pupils from families of a different faith or no faith. In most cases, the proportion is much higher, hovering in most Catholic and Church of England schools at around a third. The proportion of Catholic students in Catholic-maintained schools was around 70 per cent (75 per cent in England, 65 per cent in Wales) – in other words, numbers of non-Catholics in Catholic schools are twice what government guidelines stipulate they should be.

No faith school can turn away pupils if it has spare places. But when a school of 'religious character' is oversubscribed, it can give priority, say government guidelines, 'to children who are members of, or who practise, their faith'. To establish this, a school might ask for a reference from the family's parish priest, but they should ensure it contains no information about a parent's occupation, financial situation or educational background in case this advantages middle-class parents. Faith state schools are *religiously* selective, not *socially* selective.

Because of the popularity of church schools, many of which are oversubscribed, there has been a temptation by some schools to introduce stricter proof of pupils' parents' religious commitment. Keeping those criteria fair and simple is necessary to avoid the risk of giving some families an unfair social advantage. Privileging parents who run parish study groups or arrange the church flowers is likely, for example, to disadvantage families where both parents work. In some popular Church of England schools, for example, selection is on the basis of an elaborate points system in which frequency of church attendance and editing the parish magazine, say, will earn you extra points.

The Catholic Education Service (CES) is opposed to these complex admission arrangements, because they make it harder for the Church to provide education for the whole Catholic population, as the Butler agreement requires. Church schools are planned on the basis of being able to educate the Catholics of a local area; when one or two schools begin selecting children based on the commitment of their parents, they make it harder for local Catholic children to go there, in many cases forcing them to apply to a local non-Catholic school.

Catholic schools are required to follow the policies laid down by their diocese, which ask parents to demonstrate that they are practising Catholics according to the definition in the *Catechism* (#2041/2), namely attending Mass on Sundays; it is not for schools to impose a higher requirement of practice than the Church's own law requires.

The Joint Guidance on Admissions of the dioceses of Westminster, Southwark and Brentwood states that a Catholic is anyone who is baptised and in full communion with the Church, or who is later received into full communion. 'If there is an absolute shortage of places in the locality, a higher test of 'practising Catholic' may be employed', the Guidance notes, adding that 'the only test that is acceptable is frequency of attendance at Mass as demonstrated on the diocesan priest's reference form. It is unacceptable for schools themselves to be making judgements on pastoral matters such as Catholic practice.'

Including the transcendent

Catholic schools instil in students a sense of questioning, knowledge and respect. Through the human and natural sciences, they provide them with an understanding of aspects of human existence and deepen their grasp of the workings of the physical universe. Through religious education, they are able to explore the values and beliefs of the Catholic Church, as well as other faiths, and to seek answers to questions of origin and destiny.

The quest for the sacred – for meaning and transcendence – does not, of course, undermine the pursuit of answers through science; God 'entrusted us with the task of exploring and harnessing the mysteries of nature in order to serve a higher good,' noted Pope Benedict at Twickenham, adding: 'So it is that genuine religious belief points us beyond present utility towards the transcendent. It reminds us of the possibility and the imperative of moral conversion, of the duty to live peaceably with our neighbour, of the importance of living a life of integrity. Properly understood, it brings enlightenment, it purifies our hearts and it inspires noble and generous action, to the benefit of the entire human family.'

Or, as he earlier put it: 'A good school provides a rounded education for the whole person. And a good Catholic school, over and above this, should help all its students to become saints.'

This is why the 'Catholic ethos' of a school is much more than conformity to church doctrine. It means an education with a bigger picture. And that is good not just for the pupils and parents. It's good for Britain too.

Addressing students at Twickenham, Pope Benedict emphasised this need for breadth and openness as key to Catholic education:

> All the work you do is placed in the context of growing in friendship with God, and all that flows from that friendship. So you learn not just to be good students, but good citizens, good people. As you move higher up the school, you have to make choices regarding the subjects you study; you begin to specialise with a view to what you are going to do later in life. That is right and proper. But remember that every subject you study is part of a bigger picture. Never allow yourselves to become narrow. The world needs good scientists, but a scientific outlook becomes dangerously narrow if it ignores the religious or ethical dimension of life, just as religion becomes narrow if it rejects the legitimate contribution of science to our understanding of the world. We need good historians and philosophers and economists, but if the account they give of human life within their particular field is too narrowly focused, they can lead us seriously astray.

Existing frame

'Faith schools are divisive and harden social divisions; they encourage narrow-minded indoctrination and are inward-looking. Because they are selective and oversubscribed they can cherry-pick their students and this means children from poorer homes are under-represented.'

Reframe

Catholic schools are oases of diversity and tolerance; they instil a strong ethos of service to wider society; and the sense of identity and belonging which independent inspectors consistently applaud in them is precisely what leads to broad-minded citizens. They select religiously, not socially, which is why the pupil profile in them is more socially varied than in other schools. The schools' ethos of engagement with wider society means that pupils learn service and understanding of others.

Key messages

- Schools are an extension of the family and the community, not the state. Education is about the formation of habits and virtues; it cannot exclude the religious dimension. Serving the most disadvantaged and underprivileged has always been central to the mission of Catholic education – Catholic schools are the most ethnically diverse and international of all maintained schools in England and Wales.
- Ofsted inspection data shows that the teaching and learning, the curriculum and the quality of care, guidance and support, are all more likely to be better in

faith schools than other schools. Inspections consistently rate Catholic schools higher than average across all inspection criteria.

- Catholic schools promote diversity, tolerance and community cohesion, with students more likely to be from ethnic minorities.
- Catholic schools are more likely to be linked to local communities and are almost twice as likely as other schools to contribute to the building-up of their local community.
- Faith schools have been exempted from some aspects of equality legislation in order to preserve their freedom to be who they are. Staff in Catholic schools are generally mixed Catholic and non-Catholic, though heads are expected to be people whose belief and lifestyle is compatible with the values the school embodies.
- Far from being sectarian and divisive, Catholic schools are oases of diversity and tolerance; they instil a strong ethos of service to wider society; and the sense of identity and belonging which independent inspectors consistently applaud in them is precisely what leads to broad-minded citizens.

Chapter 7

Defending the unborn

Challenging questions
- *Would the Catholic Church want abortion to be illegal?*
- *Why does the Church put its dogma before the medical benefits of embryonic research?*
- *Surely it is a woman's right to choose?*

The Catholic Church's advocacy of unborn life is probably its best-known public position. Because of the searing and heated debates over abortion in western countries in the past decades, the Church has often found itself in the frame, an often lonely promoter of the rights of human life which contemporary society fails to recognise.

But the Church cares about unborn human life in many other areas too: wherever it is experimented on, cloned, created and killed – treated as a mere 'bunch of cells' instead of God-created early human life, deserving of respect. In recent years, the Church and pro-life groups have opposed laws allowing scientists to perform experiments on human embryos created by in-vitro fertilisation (IVF), together with embryo selection on the basis of gender and genes ('designer babies').

Because the Church has – despite the odd victory – been consistently defeated in its attempts to awaken society to the value and dignity of unborn lives, many Catholics feel powerless to alter what can seem like an inexorable slide into the dehumanisation of the unborn. And it can often seem as if the prophetic voice pointing to the humanity of the silent unborn victim – whether the 12- or 20-week-old baby destroyed by suction methods, or the cluster of human cells in the petri dish, a complete human being in its early stage – is simply ignored by a society as too disturbing. Placing an absolute value on autonomy (a woman's right to terminate a pregnancy if she chooses; the promise of cures for Parkinson's), society is growing more, not less, deaf to cries on behalf of the voiceless victims.

But Catholic Voices need a bigger view. The pattern of western cultural history, indelibly marked by Christianity, is nonetheless towards the eventual revelation of the humanity of the victim. Just as the voice of the slave, the ostracised foreigner, the battered housewife and the child abuse victim have all, eventually, been heard, so, too, western society is beginning to awaken from its deafness and is expressing greater discomfort with the prevalence and frequency of abortion, and the price that has been paid since legalisation in 1967. Empathy with the embryo – rather than the 10-week-old child in the womb – is not yet apparent to the same degree. But it is a matter of time.

On this issue therefore Catholic Voices need not accept the frame that they are opposing women's rights or scientific advance; nor need they feel obliged to assert the 'rights' of the embryo against the 'rights' of adult human beings, as if this were a question of competing claims. Rather, Catholic Voices should imagine themselves in the position of anti-slave-trade campaigners in the first years of the nineteenth century, knowing that society will eventually wake to the humanity of beings which at the moment many refuse to see.

Positive intention

Abby Johnson, the abortion clinic director turned pro-life campaigner, says in her book UnPlanned *that she 'had never been interested in promoting abortion. I'd come to Planned Parenthood eight years before, believing that its purpose was primarily to prevent unwanted pregnancies, thereby reducing the number of abortions. That had certainly been my goal. And I believed that Planned Parenthood saved lives – the lives of women who, without the services provided by this organization, might resort to some back-alley butcher.'*

Most advocates of legal abortion do not see it primarily as an ideological issue of women's rights or of personal autonomy, but as the best of alternatives. Abortion, they believe, frees a woman from an unplanned pregnancy; and keeping it legal at least prevents back-street abortions. The positive value in favour of legal abortion is therefore compassion – the same emotion which leads people to support embryonic stem-cell research on the grounds that it may lead to cures.

Life from the start

The Church has always opposed abortion, in spite of debate in the early and medieval Church about when human beings acquired souls ('ensoulment'). Punishment in canon law was graded according to whether the unborn child was unformed or formed; yet, as Professor David Albert Jones puts it, 'Even in the Middle Ages, when most Western Christians held that the early embryo was not yet fully human, it was held that the human embryo should never be attacked deliberately, however extreme the circumstances.'

This condemnation of abortion was firmly rooted in the Church's reflection on Scripture: in the Middle Ages, the main sources were Exodus and the Commandments; more recently, they draw on the Psalms, on the many instances of God forming, naming and calling the child in the womb. At the heart of the Church's advocacy is the knowledge of God as the author of our being. As the Catholic bishops of England and Wales write in their 2004 teaching document *Cherishing Life,* 'God creates each human being to be the centre of a new world that is his or her story, a whole world in miniature, a microcosm. In this sense every human being is irreplaceable.'

That is why, at the Second Vatican Council, *Gaudium et Spes* described abortion and infanticide as 'abominable crimes'.

This is a teaching about the precious value of every human life which is not of lesser value because younger and less developed. As *Cherishing Life* puts it:

> At conception or fertilisation, the fusion of the gametes from each parent produces a new

biological individual, a cell with a completely new genetic identity. From the beginning, the embryonic human exists within a network of relationships: as the offspring of a mother and a father and as the gift of God the creator. Each embryo is a living being, possessing the dynamic potential to develop, in interaction with his or her mother, passing through many stages of development first inside the womb and then outside. The qualities we think of as being most distinctively human do not show themselves until much later in life. However, we should not judge things only by how they appear at one particular time; we must also consider what they have in them to become. Babies are human beings before they can walk and talk, even though many of their abilities have not yet become fully apparent. With an embryo we are considering the very earliest stages of human development, but the principle is the same. The humanity of the embryo shows itself as he or she grows and develops. What is hidden and mysterious unfolds and becomes evident with time. The human embryo should therefore be regarded as 'not a potential human being but a human being with potential'.

Abortion as eugenics

The abortion question is really two: the wrongness/ licitness of abortion itself; and what the law and the state should determine. Unlike the US, abortion is not a party-political question in the UK; when MPs vote on abortion, they usually do so according to conscience, rather than according to their party's policy. For the Church to call on Parliament to review the abortion laws is not, therefore, intervening in politics to favour one party over another; and when the Church – as it always does – makes that same call prior to every general election it is not sending out a coded message about whom to vote for. There is no such thing as a 'pro-life party' among the three main parties; all of them have their pro-life lobbies and wings, made up predominantly of Christians.

Few argue that abortion is a moral good, but most believe that making it illegal would be worse: they will say that unplanned pregnancies are inevitable, and that women who seek to end them should not be criminalised or forced into the hands of back-alley butchers. This was the argument in favour of the 1967 Act, although the effect – as even the law's architects admit – has been to go far beyond decriminalising the desperate acts of women seeking back-street terminations, to a point where abortion is now a socially acceptable (even if seldom discussed) back-up to failed contraception. Of the 189,574 women aborting their children in England and Wales in 2010, about a third (64,303) had had a previous abortion or abortions. The cost to the National Health Service of providing abortions in 2009–10 was £86.2 million.

Abortion has always been linked to eugenics: the decision to terminate a pregnancy is frequently made after learning that a baby is disabled, often in the hospital where a woman discovers a disability through a pre-natal scan. Hospital staff will often suggest it at this point, and the abortion is carried out as a matter of routine; few people will ever know about it. In this way, the termination of those society deems unfit or burdensome is being carried out daily, on a very large scale – thus fulfilling, by a series of individual choices, the ambitions of the early twentieth-century eugenicists.

Referring to both abortion and the selection of embryos by in-vitro fertilisation techniques(IVF), Cardinal Cormac Murphy-O'Connor wrote in 2005: '[the] terrible truth is that it is the strong who decide the fate of the weak.' Noting the six million abortions carried out in the UK since 1967, the Cardinal wrote: 'Human beings … become instruments of other human beings. That way lies eugenics, and we know from German history where that leads. We are already on that road: for what else is the termination of six million lives in the womb since the Abortion Act was introduced, and embryo selection on the basis of gender and genes?'

The link between eugenics and abortion should not surprise us. In 1992, on the twenty-fifth anniversary of the Act, its architect, Lord Steele, paid tribute to the role of the Abortion Law Reform Association (ALRA) in getting his bill through. ALRA was founded in the 1930s by women closely linked to the Eugenics Society, a group committed to the poorer having fewer children. And indeed abortion, notes Dennis Sewell in *The Political Gene*, 'has had a greater impact in reducing births among the economically disadvantaged than the middle class, and is proportionately more frequently carried out on women from racial minorities in the United States.'

The mass extermination of the disabled unborn was brought home in the UK in 2001 as a result of a highly unusual legal challenge by an Anglican vicar. In the UK, unlike in the US, abortions are illegal after 24 weeks' pregnancy – unless the child in the womb is considered to have a 'serious handicap'. What constitutes a serious handicap is shrouded in mystery (the reasons for carrying out abortions are confidential); nor is there any legal definition of 'serious handicap'.

But as the Revd Joanna Jepson's case demonstrated, the term covers deformities easily corrected by surgery, such as a cleft palate. Between 1995 and late 2003, 26 abortions on foetuses with cleft palates took place in the United Kingdom, two of them after 24 weeks. Jepson, who was herself born with a cleft palate (corrected by an operation in her teens), argued that the abortion of a 28-week-old baby carried out in December 2001 in Hertfordshire was 'unlawful killing'. The complaint was not upheld; the Crown Prosecution Service said the doctors had acted in good faith and would not face criminal charges.

Yet there has also been a growing reaction against the prevalence and ease of access to abortion. A 2006 survey published in the *Observer* ('Choose Life 2006 Survey of Public Opinion'), the broadest and most in-depth study of attitudes of UK women towards abortion for many years, showed a clear majority of two-thirds in favour of reforming the law to make abortion far more restrictive. (Incidentally, this poll, along with others, shows women are far more knowledgeable than men about life in the womb, and far more anti-abortion – a point often ignored by those claiming abortion to be a 'gender' issue.) The poll also showed that British people think it unacceptable that abortion is legal up to birth on grounds of disability. So far, Parliament has resisted moves to reform the UK's abortion law; the last attempt, at the time of the 2008 Human Fertilisation and Embryology Bill, failed.

However, the ground of the abortion debate has shifted markedly in the last five to ten years, away from a zero-sum clash between the 'right to choose' and the 'right to life'. Increasingly, studies reveal the harm done by abortion to women as well as men, who may suffer searing grief and regret for many years afterwards. And what science itself is revealing is the humanity of the unborn child.

A growing empathy

The so-called 'Walking in the womb' 4D ultrasound films by Professor Stuart Campbell, made public in 2004, have helped to shift public opinion. Campbell, an atheist, pro-choice doctor who used to perform abortions, is very far from being a pro-life campaigner; yet, as a result of what he has seen through ultrasound technology, he has become an outspoken advocate of reducing the legal upper limit. At the point where 30 per cent of abortions are carried out – between 10 and 12 weeks – the unborn child can clearly be seen 'smiling', 'walking' and feeling pain: a fully formed human being. Developments in ultrasound technology have made it impossible, now, to conceal what an abortion actually involves.

Because the legal upper limit has been traditionally determined by the idea of 'viability' – that is, when life can be sustained outside the womb, independent of the mother – advances in medical technology led in 1990 to a reduction in the legal upper limit from 28 to 24 weeks. Advances since then have led to calls for reducing the legal upper limit from 24 weeks (the legal maximum in the UK, one of the most liberal in the world) to 12 weeks, which is the norm in Europe. The 'viability' argument shows that even in Britain, where abortion laws are permissive, a woman's 'right' to abort the child in her womb is curtailed by what is, in effect, a recognition of the humanity of the unborn child; the law accepts that unborn life has rights, but is unable to agree the point at which those rights can be asserted at the expense of other rights. Hence the attempt to use 'viability' as a 'scientific' measure; but what the science actually says is, of course, disputed, and harnessed to political and ethical views. Do we leave it to science to determine what we value, when science itself claims not to be concerned with what is right and wrong but what is verifiable?

Catholic bishops favour (and are) working for the step-by-step reduction in the legal upper limit as a gradual process. To re-criminalise abortion is an unrealistic political ambition; Parliament would only do so is in response to public opinion. But much can be done in the meantime to restrict abortion. As Cardinal Murphy-O'Connor explained in 2007, 'It is both licit and important for those in public life who oppose abortion to work and vote for achievable and incremental improvements to an unjust law.' The pro-life movement, of which the Catholic Church is the largest and most important player, works actively to persuade Parliament to make abortions rarer, and to give greater status and greater protection for the human embryo.

But the Church's opposition to abortion is not *solely* concerned with reform of the law by an Act of Parliament. The open letter by Cardinals Cormac Murphy-

O'Connor and Keith O'Brien on the fortieth anniversary of the 1967 Abortion Act emphasises the need to create genuine alternatives for pregnant women (in addition to, or complementary to, efforts to reduce the legal upper limit). The Life charity, for example, offers housing and education to pregnant women as well as advice and guidance. Its slogan, 'loving life, offering hope', shows that the life movement is increasingly a social, or civic, one, rather than solely a political or philosophical one. This allows us also to frame the life movement as not merely saying 'no' to abortion but saying a big 'yes' – to a society in which life is embraced and welcomed.

Embryo research

In the run-up to Parliament debating the Human Fertilisation and Embryology Bill in 2008, it was repeatedly claimed that the creation and cloning of human embryos (creating human – animal hybrids) would enable cures for Alzheimer's, Parkinson's and other diseases. Those who opposed the legalisation of this new development in the disrespect of human life were depicted as religious fanatics putting obstacles in the path of medical progress. Science, we were told, needed the greatest freedom for success; and the UK, already a world leader in stem-cell research, needed a law that would unfetter its research laboratories and so help usher in a new generation of seemingly astonishing cures.

For sufferers of those ailments, this was irresponsible hype and a cruel deception. In reality, embryonic stem-cell research has resulted in no significant medical developments. There are no treatments derived from embryonic stem cells. On the other hand, there are literally dozens of treatments involving adult stem cells (extracted from bone marrow or placentas), which are entirely ethical. Stem-cell science is indeed at the cutting edge of medical research; there have been huge strides made in creating new organs from stem cells. Yet none of these has involved *embryonic* stem cells. Lord Robert Winston, the fertility pioneer, admitted in 2008 that it was 'no great shakes' if scientists were not allowed to engineer hybrids. As a number of leading stem-cell scientists wrote in a letter to *The Times* at the time of the Bill, 'such proposals are highly speculative in comparison to established sources of human stem cells and we remain unaware of any cogent evidence suggesting any might yield significant therapeutic dividend'. There was no compelling therapeutic case, in other words, for embryonic research.

The demand for it comes from private medical research companies seeking funding. To attract backers, they need constantly to dangle the possibility of 'breakthroughs' as a result of cutting-edge, blue-sky experiments. Their interest is in expanding the possibilities of what they can do in the laboratory in the hope that at some point an unforeseen development will occur. The momentum in 2008 came from the furious lobbying of the pharmaceuticals and Britain's largest charity, the Wellcome Trust, which funds much of the research. They have lobbied hard for the freedom to explore all options so that *at the end of the road* miracle cures will be available. Privately many scientists say the arguments of the lobby are highly questionable, but they are afraid to speak out because their institutions would lose the huge grants on which they depend.

The passage of the 2008 Act marked the victory of a dogma – the notion that scientific enquiry should be unconstrained – over the traditional idea that tampering with human life for medical purposes requires a compelling ethical justification. The ethical duty society owes to human life requires a stringent scrutiny of claims of possible benefits. The Church proposes an ethical calculus – a reasoned examination of the ethics weighed against the anticipated benefits – while the medical research lobby has been resorting to an entirely unreasonable claim to be free of any such calculus. Good science has always been accompanied by ethical standards. Ethics is good for science: standards and trust are key.

This argument is often framed as science versus religion, or religion versus medicine. Catholics are sometimes asked in studios by sufferers of terminal diseases what they have to say to them: 'How can you sit there and oppose what could make me better?' The answer is that they have been sold a lie; that adult stem-cell research is far more likely to produce a cure for them. The newspapers may be talking about breakthroughs from embryonic research; the scientific journals are not.

Yet it is not because embryonic research has failed to produce the much-hyped cures that it is wrong. A human embryo is the first stage of life; to use human life as the subject of experimentation is to desecrate that life. The fact that researchers use embryos left over from IVF treatment which would be anyway destroyed in no way detracts from the essential wrongness of experimenting on human life.

Few would maintain that the cluster of cells that makes up an embryo is morally equivalent to other clusters of cells – cancerous cells, say, or the embryo of a rat. If the embryo were so regarded, there would be no need, for example, for Parliament to create a Human Fertilisation and Embryology Authority (HFEA) to regulate research on human embryos and to consider the ethical dilemmas involved. This body was set up in the wake of the first HFE Act in 1990 to grant licences to researchers and IVF clinicians who wished to make use of new technologies such as the screening of embryos for certain genetic characteristics. Although the 1990 Act fell short of recognising the embryo as human life – which it could hardly have done, given the abortion law – it accorded the embryo a 'special status' and imposed constraints: human embryos should be used only if the research was justifiable; and only embryos younger than 14 days could be used (before the 'primitive streak' develops, the nerve tissue that is the first indication of the capacity for thought). But that has not, in practice, meant a lot. The HFEA has almost never turned down an application for a research licence.

Other countries take the protection of the embryo far more seriously than the UK. Following the 2008 HFE Act, a number of Britain's neighbours expressed strong reservations about the way it had ignored the need to weigh ethical reservations about the use of human life against the anticipated benefits of research. The German Medical Association, for example, said that the British were 'developing a completely different relationship to growing life'.

Surplus embryos

In-vitro fertilisation (IVF) creates many surplus embryos which are then frozen or destroyed or used for medical experiments. Inherent in the technique is selecting an embryo for implantation in the womb. This power has led, inevitably, to calls to allow embryos to be selected for particular characteristics: gender, hair colour, and so on.

The 2008 Act also allowed the selection of an embryo that grows into a child with a particular tissue type, if the family needs that tissue to help treat a sibling with a particular disease. These so-called 'saviour siblings' would bring into the world, said the then Archbishop of Cardiff, Peter Smith, children 'who may be loved, but who have been born in order to be donors'.

People are not ends. As the Archbishop of Canterbury, Rowan Williams, wrote at the time, in most people's understanding of what counts as moral behaviour, it is taken for granted that you don't use anyone else just for your own purposes – or even for other people's purposes. 'A human person, an individual body with feelings and thoughts, needs to be treated, as we sometimes say, as an end in itself, not a tool for someone else's agenda. So we condemn rape, torture and blackmail. We don't allow experiments on people's bodies or minds without their consent. And we don't breed human individuals to create a pool of organs that could be transplanted to save the lives of others.'

'Saviour siblings' and other forms of embryo selection use the technique known as pre-implantation genetic diagnosis (PGD), in which embryos are selected on the basis of a particular gene. The Vatican instruction *Dignitas Personae* deplores this as a form of eugenics:

Pre-implantation diagnosis – connected as it is with artificial fertilisation, which is itself always intrinsically illicit – is directed toward the *qualitative selection and consequent destruction of embryos,* which constitutes an act of abortion. Pre-implantation diagnosis is therefore the expression of a *eugenic mentality* that accepts selective abortion in order to prevent the birth of children affected by various types of anomalies. Such an attitude is shameful and utterly reprehensible, since it presumes to measure the value of a human life only within the parameters of 'normality' and physical well-being, thus opening the way to legitimizing infanticide and euthanasia as well.

The existing frame

'Most people in this country believe the right to an abortion should be enshrined in law. If the Church had its way, there would be a return to back-street abortion.

Research on embryos that are just a cluster of cells and not viable gives the hope of finding a cure for terrible diseases. How is having a second child (so-called 'saviour sibling'), who can give stem cells to save their brother or sister, wrong?'

Reframe

The Catholic Church speaks on behalf of the voiceless, defenceless embryo, just as it speaks on behalf of other 'silent' victims. The Church seeks to bring down the upper legal limit on abortion in order to reach a point where abortion is no longer practised. At the same time, the Church seeks to promote public awareness of the fragility and value of unborn life and to offer real choices to women frightened of unplanned or unwanted pregnancies. The Church wants to work towards creating a society where all life is welcomed and valued.

Embryos are the early stage of human life; they are vulnerable and need protection from the law. The real good news is the rapid progress made in adult stem-cell research. All the major developments have been in adult stem cells, not embryonic ones. Claims made for embryonic stem-cell research are exaggerated and wishful – the result of hype by corporations and research labs seeking publicity and funding.

Key messages

- The good news is the rapid progress made in adult stem-cell research. All the major developments have been in adult stem cells, not embryonic ones. Claims made for embryonic stem-cell research are exaggerated and wishful thinking – the result of hype by corporations and research labs seeking publicity and funding.
- The Catholic Church is a major investor in adult stem-cell research – Vatican labs, Catholic hospitals, etc.
- All science is governed by an ethical framework – good science and good ethics go together (embryonic stem-cell research has been marred by scandals: it is dangerous).

- There are powerful corporate interests behind embryonic stem-cell research. Unborn life is a powerless plaything in the hands of those interests.
- Even Britain, with its cowboy, loosely regulated science environment, accords the embryo 'special status' and demands that embryos used for research must be destroyed after 14 days – this is not just a bunch of cells.
- Embryos are the early stage of human life; they are vulnerable and need protection by the law.
- The worth of human life is not linked to its appearance or size – because an embryo is tiny makes it no less human life, and worthy of care and protection.
- Britain has a casual attitude towards embryos. Compare with other leading European countries which are much more strictly regulated. Disrespect for embryos signals a wider disrespect for human life, which is morally corrosive.
- There is a moral awakening in British society – a growing awareness of the wonder and beauty of unborn life – which is being ignored by Parliament. The Catholic Church speaks on behalf of the voiceless, defenceless embryo, just as it speaks on behalf of other 'silent' victims.

Chapter 8

Catholics and AIDS

Challenging questions

- *Why doesn't the Church recognise that effective use of condoms would save millions of lives in Africa?*
- *When many men working away from home are infected by prostitutes and then infect their wives when they go home, how can the Church forbid the use of condoms?*
- *Shouldn't prostitutes and others not ready to embrace chastity be encouraged to use condoms?*
- *Has the Pope recently backtracked on the Church's absolute ban on condoms?*

The world may be adept at overlooking the plight of Africa, but no one can ignore the HIV/AIDS pandemic, the greatest threat to the continent since the slave trade. It seems obvious to most people in western countries that, just as the widespread use of condoms contributed to bringing down rates of HIV transmission among gay men in the US and Western Europe in the 1980s, the 'answer' to AIDS in Africa must be more of the same. Yet HIV (the virus that causes AIDS) in Africa has different characteristics, and a deluge of evidence points to the ineffectiveness of campaigns encouraging people to have 'safe sex'.

The Church's alternative policy – encouraging responsible sexual behaviour, while tackling stigma and poverty
– is born not just of moral conviction but of knowledge of
the realities of Africa on the ground. To the secular
western mind, however, it seems just the opposite: the
imposition by detached dogmatists of a religious doctrine. As a result, Catholics find themselves admonished
for 'contributing to the spread of the virus', 'sacrificing
innocent lives on the altar of dogma', and even 'being
directly responsible for the deaths of millions of Africans'.

Catholic Voices therefore have a large task of reframing. But once the facts are examined, it is clear that it is
the 'more condoms' approach which betrays a detached,
even colonialist, mentality; abstinence programmes, on
the other hand, have a proven track record of success in
curbing the spread of the virus. As is now finally being
accepted, the early strategy of the UNAIDS programme
was based on a fatal misreading of African realities; the
approach which had worked so well in the 1980s in
Europe and the US, it turned out, was quite inappropriate for Africa, while precisely those programmes which
aimed at behaviour change have proved to be the most
successful – the kind of programmes which the Catholic
Church (among others) had argued were the key to
defeating AIDS.

In his 2003 book *Rethinking AIDS Prevention*, the
anthropologist and Harvard expert Edward C. Green
attributes this disaster to the mindset of the mainly
European and American health experts who advise governments on their policies for combating AIDS. Many of
today's international health bureaucracies were estab-

lished in the 1970s, when the governments of rich countries, fearing population explosion in poor countries,
poured money into programmes to promote contraception. When AIDS began to spread in the 1980s, therefore, it was easy to deploy these same methods to combat
the virus – especially as condoms had proved effective in
reducing AIDS among promiscuous groups in the US
and Europe. But the causes of the rapid spread of African
AIDS were very different, as we shall see.

The Church, which has argued against those flawed
strategies from the start, knew this. No other organisation has had such intense involvement on the frontline of
prevention and treatment in sub-Saharan Africa and
other developing countries; no single civil society organisation can match the Church's presence and activity in
both the prevention and treatment of HIV among the
poor, and especially among the most remote villages and
in the poorest slums. That pervasive presence hardly
makes it 'detached' from the realities in Africa, as some
critics have held. Other critics agree that the Catholic
presence and influence are enormous, but use that fact
to blame the Church for failing to include condoms as
part of its HIV prevention strategy. But this criticism
wrongly assumes that condoms are the key to combating
AIDS in Africa.

The question turns, therefore, on the 'effectiveness' of
condoms in combating HIV. There is plenty of hard
evidence that condoms-based campaigns against HIV in
sub-Saharan Africa, where 22.5 million people (about
two-thirds of the world's total) are infected, have failed to
contain the spread of the virus, for reasons we will come
on to; and in most cases, the evidence shows, have

aggravated it. However the issue is not so straightforward, because it is also true that the use of condoms has been effective – although not as effective as partner reduction – in reducing transmission among high-risk groups such as prostitutes. In this sense, therefore, neither the statement 'condoms are effective in reducing HIV transmission' nor 'condoms are ineffective in reducing HIV transmission' is per se true. What the science shows is that, in the African population at large, behaviour change is the key factor in reducing virus transmission; and by encouraging risky behaviour, condom campaigns cause transmission rates to increase. On the other hand, among groups engaging in highly risky behaviour who are not ready or willing to change, condoms may cause transmission rates to decrease. But this is a very small population compared to the first.

To add to the confusion, there have been concerns raised by some African bishops in the past – and even, at one stage, by a Vatican cardinal – that condoms are 'porous' and do not, in fact, act as a barrier to the transmission of the virus. These claims are not supported by the evidence; the paper which attempted to present that case, published in 2004 by Cardinal Alfonso López Trujillo, then head of the Council for the Family at the Vatican, was widely derided, and has been allowed to quietly drop. Because the paper received extensive media treatment, however, when church leaders – including, notably, Pope Benedict in 2009 – assert the ineffectiveness of condom-based strategies against HIV in the wider population, they are often wrongly heard as claiming that condoms are porous, and met with derision. But as Pope

Benedict knew very well, condoms have proved ineffective against AIDS in Africa – but not because they are 'porous'.

The key assumption that dogs this discussion – and the flaw in the strategy of the international agencies up until relatively recently – is the persistent myth that what worked to bring down HIV rates in Europe and the US – namely, widespread condom use within the most vulnerable population, gay men – will also bring it down in Africa, where HIV is spread mainly through heterosexual intercourse.

But after two decades, the failure of this 'technical' strategy is clear: HIV transmission rates in Africa soared between 1990 and 2005, as international organisations pumped billions into promoting condom use. It is therefore the Church's assertion, that AIDS will only be defeated by behaviour change, and by addressing the conditions which make AIDS in Africa different from developed northern countries, which now looks like a far stronger case.

The story has been fuelled by warm discussions among moral theologians and church leaders on the narrower question of whether, in the case of people unready or unable to embrace monogamy, fidelity and abstinence, it is incumbent upon the Church to urge them to use condoms as prophylactics, where the intention is to prevent death rather than life. Pope Benedict intervened in this discussion in November 2010. In *Light of the World* he cited the case of a prostitute who chooses to use a condom in order to avoid infecting the other, and interpreted this act of care as the possible beginning of a journey of moral awakening. The Pope's few lines in the interview were later clarified in a statement from the Congregation for the Doctrine of the Faith, which allows us now to state the Church's position with greater precision.

Positive intention

Millions of people are in danger of being infected in Africa and sooner or later dying of AIDS . Children are being left orphaned, migrant workers are having sex with infected prostitutes and then coming home and infecting their wives. So the Church seems both distant and heartless when it says that condom use is not the solution but part of the problem, and dogmatic to suggest that abstinence and fidelity are better solutions. Shouldn't the Church be willing to accept condom use, even at the risk of condoning adultery, fornication and other abuses, or apparently violating church teaching against artificial contraception within marriage? Should it not prefer 'to save lives' than to sacrifice them in order to defend its teaching?

'The Church has AIDS'

The Catholic and Protestant Churches have been running outstanding AIDS programmes in Africa since the 1980s. No organisation has been closer to, and more involved with, the communities afflicted by AIDS than the Catholic Church. And no organisation has been more effective in tackling AIDS at its root.

Along with Protestant Churches, the Catholics were on the 'front lines' as soon as the epidemic began, responding to the imperative to care for the suffering and dying and to educate the human family in ways to prevent the further spread of HIV. Today, often in partnership with others, they play a vital and expanding role in the comprehensive response to HIV across the developing world: assisting people in avoiding infection; providing tests to find out if they are infected; offering physical and spiritual care to those who are; working in communities to combat stigmatisation and discrimination; caring for those affected (especially widows and orphans); helping those infected to 'live positively'; and advocating on behalf of persons living with HIV or AIDS (NB: never 'AIDS victims'). This large-scale service of a suffering population has given rise to theological reflection. So closely do Catholics identify with those infected that some speak of the Church itself 'living with AIDS'.

Catholic AIDS programmes work through existing diocesan/parish structures; they do not come from 'outside', but are part of the Church's everyday mission – which is why they are valued by international agencies for both their compassion and effectiveness. The great strength of the Catholic response to AIDS is that the Church is not an NGO providing a service for the people; the Church *is* the people. As Bishop Kevin Dowling of Rustenberg, former chair of the Southern African Catholic Bishops' Conference (SACBC)'s AIDS office, puts it, the Church's response 'is intimately linked to its mission in the world, a response which must be based on and reveal fundamental Gospel attitudes, values such as compassion, solidarity, care for the vulnerable, striving for justice and commitment to overcoming unjust structures in society'. Bishop Dowling goes on to list the practical actions which flow from this:

> We stand with, we want to be with the little ones, the people who do not count, who will never be listened to because they are not given access to anything or any structure; those who are lost in some outlying community or urban slum which will rarely, if ever, be visited by anyone; the little ones who end up simply being a number, a statistic, whether it be in terms of the escalating infection rate or in terms of the escalating numbers of dead in the mortuaries awaiting a pauper's funeral, sometimes for months on end because families cannot be traced. We want to be with the poorest and alienated communities, to be present to and involved with them in their reality.

Leaving aside its many other qualifications to speak on this issue, therefore, the number and reach of its programmes mean the Church deserves to be recognised as possibly the world's leading voice on AIDS. Yet consistently it has been sidelined from the debate over the international community's response to the virus because of its 'dogmatic' opposition to contraception.

According to UNAIDS (2010), about 22.5 million sub-Saharan Africans are infected – nearly 70 per cent of the total global population of 33.3 million living with HIV. Between 2000 and 2020, about 55 million Africans will have died of AIDS-related diseases. The pandemic has decimated the population, wiping out in many areas half of the working-age people, leaving grandparents to care for their orphan grandchildren.

Vatican officials estimate that around the world the Church ministers to more than 25 per cent of all those with HIV/AIDS. In Africa, that figure rises to 50 or 75 per cent – and, in many remote areas, close to 100 per cent.

The Southern African bishops' (SABC) AIDS Office, founded in 2000, coordinates more than 150 programmes in the region which prevent and treat AIDS. It runs a vast network of hospitals, clinics, hospices, home-based care projects and orphanages, and has pioneered programmes for women and young people, educating and enabling them to resist sexual advances. Literally hundreds of thousands of people in South Africa, Namibia, Swaziland, Botswana and Lesotho have received training and support from Catholic programmes. Dozens of Catholic schools teach HIV prevention in their curricula.

Given that half of new HIV infections are found among the 15–24-year-old age group, the SACBC AIDS Office has focused on young adults in particular. Its programmes develop attitudes of commitment and responsibility in sexual behaviour, making young people aware of the unequal power relationship between men and women and ways in which they can promote and advance their equal dignity. Its three other priorities are: (1) community-based care for the sick and dying, and care for orphans; (2) programmes of education and awareness which tackle the silence and the stigma attached to HIV, encouraging people to be tested and to talk about the virus; and (3) combating the poverty and ignorance which often lie at the root of the spread of HIV.

Why are so many young people infected? The AIDS Office identifies the following reasons: (1) migrant labour, and the fragmentation of families; (2) extreme poverty, which forces young women into the sex trade; (3) vulnerable teenagers, orphaned by parents dying in large numbers from AIDS, made to have sex with relatives; and (4) the bombardment of young people with the message – sponsored by international organisations – that it is fine to have sex, as long as they do it 'safely'.

The AIDS Office's chief prevention programme for young people is called 'Education for Life'. Originally developed by Catholics in Uganda, where it is credited with significantly reducing the rate of new infections there, it stresses long-term abstinence and life long and mutual fidelity among spouses. The programme is summed up as 'ABCD': 'Abstain, Be faithful, Change your lifestyle, or you are in Danger of contracting HIV.'

Another key element of the prevention programme is the testing of pregnant mothers and the use of anti-retroviral drugs to prevent mother-to-baby transmission. The Catholic Church is exceptional in Southern Africa in the extent of its provision to the sick and the dying. Its network of hospices has expanded to meet the vast demand from people living with AIDS. Its clinics offer nutrition and antiretroviral treatment.

The AIDS Office also advocates for legal reform on issues related to people living with or affected by HIV, particularly with regards to children's rights; in advocating for free education for orphans and disability grants for the sick; and in expanding access to antiretroviral drugs. Its projects seek to overcome stigma and prejudice towards people living with, or affected by, HIV within parishes.

In short, the Catholic Church in Southern Africa has the infrastructure, the passion, the resources, the expertise, the experience and the dedication to confront the challenge of AIDS. Its prevention programmes are highly effective in educatingyoung people to resist sexual advances, and to abstain until marriage. A large part of the effectiveness of the Church's anti-HIV programmes lies in their community-based approach, depending on a large network of volunteers with strong values and a dedication to helping others.

The (in)effectiveness of condom-based campaigns

Condom use is only effective in reducing HIV transmission within identifiable sub-groups (prostitutes, gay men), not in the population at large, where it has the opposite effect: evidence correlates the greater availability and use of condoms with higher infection rates. There are many reasons for this, not least the idea of risk compensation implicit in the idea of 'safe' sex. Just as, in the West, the removal of the fear of unwanted pregnancies through widespread contraception has led to the average age of first sexual encounter coming down year on year, so in Africa condoms campaigns have sent the message to young people that it's okay to have sex. This 'risk compensation' or 'behavioural disinhibition' is what has fuelled the spread of the virus, according to one of the world's leading experts on AIDS, Dr Edward C. Green of Harvard University. 'People take more sexual risks', he says, 'because they feel safer than is actually justified when using condoms.'

Another reason is that condom use is simply not consistent or prevalent enough, in spite of massive promotions, to reduce the virus – a consequence of poor infrastructure and transportation networks and other aspects of poverty. In a 9 May 2008 article for *Science* magazine, ten AIDS experts concluded that 'consistent condom use has not reached a sufficiently high level, even after many years of widespread and often aggressive promotion, to produce a measurable slowing of the new infections in the generalized epidemics of sub-saharan Africa.' The biggest chunk of the US$3.2 billion UNAIDS budget has been allocated to condoms-based interventions which are 'unsupported by rigorous evidence', they add, noting that only 20 per cent has been directed at generalised epidemics in Africa, and a negligible part of that budget has been directed at changing sexual behaviour.

Yet it is clear, say those experts, that 'partner reduction' is the key to curbing AIDS. Helen Epstein, a public health researcher, is the author of a highly-praised 2007 book on the virus. *The Invisible Cure* showed how 'concurrency' – having multiple, long-term sexual partners – was the key reason why HIV rates were increasing in Africa despite increased condom use. Although the evidence for this was everywhere, the reluctance to translate it into international policies aimed at partner reduction, as her book devastatingly shows, has everything to do with a reluctance on the part of western liberals to introduce programmes of moral behaviour that would challenge their own values.

'Concurrency' is the name given to a particularly African form of infidelity. In Europe and the US, promiscuity is associated with casual sex (one-off liaisons, uncommitted relationships); in Africa, however, the main vehicle for the rapid escalation of the virus has been the prevalence of committed, long-term multiple relationships which act as a kind of 'superhighway' for the virus. As she puts it: 'AIDS is common in Africa not because African people have so many sexual partners, but because they are more likely than people in other world regions to have a small number of concurrent long-term partners. This places them, along with their partner or partners, within a vast network of ongoing sexual relationships that is highly conducive to the spread of HIV'.

As Epstein also shows, there are many other, interlocking and multifaceted, reasons for the prevalence of 'concurrency': the imbalance of power between genders; war and instability; forced migration alcohol abuse and pervasive violence. The vulnerability of the poor in Africa causes them to seek protection in long-term sexual relationships. The key factor, therefore, is a particular form of promiscuity which means that, while Africans are not more promiscuous than people elsewhere, the particular form of that promiscuity creates a 'virus superhighway' which explains the explosion of AIDS in Africa.

While condoms are effective in reducing the spread of the virus in casual sexual encounters, they are seldom used in long-term, stable relationships, which is where most of the AIDS transmission in Africa occurs. Unsurprisingly, 'it turns out that partner reduction has played a key role wherever HIV rates have fallen,' notes Epstein, but this is especially true of Africa. In Zimbabwe and

Kenya, for example, the HIV rate began to decline in the late 1990s as numbers of multiple partnerships fell; but in Botswana, South Africa and Lesotho, where no partner reduction occurred in the 1990s and where condoms were emphasised as the main method of prevention, HIV rates soared.

Why have international organisations been so slow to recognise this, and to urge sexual behaviour change? Until 2006 no public health programme in Southern Africa informed people of the dangers of concurrency, and the topic was absent from the policy documents of every international public health organisation. Instead, the 'fixation' – as the Pope calls it – on condoms, with the assumption that increasing use will reduce infection, has been driven 'not by evidence, but by ideology, stereotypes and false assumptions', according to Dr Green. That ideology had everything to with UNAIDS officials moving into AIDS from family planning, where the notion of a policy based on morality was anathema. At the 2005 international AIDS conference in Bangkok, researchers presenting evidence about the importance of fidelity in AIDS prevention were accused of 'moralizing' and 'practically booed off stage', notes Epstein.

Dr Green – himself an agnostic scientist – was one of a handful of experts who for years had been arguing that faithfulness was key to combatting the virus. Sidelined and ignored in the 1990s, they now represent mainstream scientific opinion, although the western media – reflecting ignorance of the evidence in wider society – has been slow to catch on: hence the hailstorm of outrage which met Benedict XVI when, on his way to Cameroon in March 2009, he told journalists that AIDS is 'a tragedy that cannot be overcome by money alone, and that cannot be overcome by the distribution of condoms, which even aggravates the problems'.

Dr Green – the author of five books and 250 peer-reviewed articles – said the Pope was 'actually correct': condoms-based campaigns, he said, 'result in efforts that are at best ineffective and at worst harmful'.

Another 'lone voice', James Shelton of the US Agency for International Development, also agreed with Benedict XVI; as he wrote in *The Lancet,* 'condoms alone have limited impact in generalised epidemics'. And indeed, no country in Africa has yet turned back a generalised epidemic by means of condom distribution. In Cameroon, to where the Pope was travelling when he made his remarks, between 1992 and 2001 condom sales increased from 6 million to 15 million while HIV infection rates trebled, from 3 per cent to 9 per cent.

As Fr Michael Czerny, former director of the African Jesuit AIDS Network (AJAN) puts it, 'The promotion of condoms as the strategy for reducing HIV infection in a general population is based on statistical probability and intuitive plausibility. It enjoys considerable credibility in the Western media and among Western opinion makers. What it lacks is scientific support.'

Condoms-based campaigns carry an implicit pessimism about human beings, seeing people as rapacious, unable to control themselves, and incapable of moving beyond self-gratification. It is a pessimistic attitude, one alien to traditional African values. Imposed by international agencies on Africans, it represents, says Fr Czerny, an 'unconscious racism'.

The Church's approach – gained from experience on the ground, among some of the poorest communities in Africa, blighted by AIDS – is that the virus must be tackled in two key ways.

The first is through the 'humanisation of sexuality', based on faith in God and respect for oneself and others, in contrast to the 'banalisation of sexuality' implicit in condom campaigns. Sound epidemiological research supports the Church's approach. As Dr Green writes: 'As evidence mounts about the high prevalence and deadly nature of multiple and concurrent partnerships, we must reorient prevention interventions and research to promote behaviour change – in particular, partner reduction and sexual exclusivity.' The classic example is Uganda, where HIV prevalence declined from 21 per cent to 9.8 per cent in the 1990s following a reduction in concurrent (non-regular) sexual partners by 65 per cent. That shift in behaviour was the result of a government-backed, community-based campaign supported by the Churches.

The campaign did not exclude condoms, but it was behaviour change, according to Low-Beer and Stoneburner (2004), which was the crucial factor. 'There was a wide range of sexual behaviour changes in Uganda: reducing partners, abstinence, faithfulness, marriage, increased condom use, as well as others we probably will never know about … The major difference in Uganda is a reduction in non-regular sexual partners and an associated contraction of sexual networks.' In July 2010 UNAIDS announced significant reductions in rates of transmission among young people as a result of behaviour change. According to a Reuters report, 'the study found the main drivers of the reductions were changes in sexual behaviour. Young people in 13 of the 25 countries were waiting longer before they become sexually active. In more than half of the 25 countries, young people were choosing to have fewer sexual partners.'

This approach is the most effective, the most realistic, and the most successful. Nor is there an alternative. As the Catholic bishops of Africa put it in their message at the end of the II Synod for Africa (October 2009): 'The problem cannot be overcome by the distribution of prophylactics. We appeal to all who are genuinely interested in arresting the sexual transmission of HIV to recognise the success of programmes that propose abstinence among those not yet married, and fidelity among the married. Such a course not only offers the best protection against the spread of this disease but is also in harmony with Christian morality.'

The second part of the Church's approach is described by Pope Benedict in *Light of the World* as assisting people 'up close and concretely' through 'prevention, education, help, counsel and accompaniment'. People can only change their behaviour with support from those who are willing to come alongside them, offering solace and assistance. Despair is the enemy of change. Faith is its friend. A Church which tirelessly serves those in need is credible in the teaching and formation it offers.

High-risk groups and condoms: what does the Church say?

Because of the large numbers of Catholics living with AIDS, and because the Church's outreach to the infected excludes no one, the Church has been faced over the years with the ethical question of whether it is up to the Church to give information about the use of condoms to people engaging in high-risk sexual behaviour who are unable or not ready to change that behaviour.

Distributing condoms is out of the question: that would be to exacerbate the problem already outlined, and undermine the Church's message. (As Pope Benedict says in *Light of the World*, 'people can get condoms when they want anyway'). The question has been whether Catholic pastoral practice can include urging a man or woman who is infected or engaging in high-risk sexual behaviour to protect themselves or others. Some maintain that this would be to condone harmful and sinful behaviour, and/or advocate artificial contraception which is forbidden in *Humanae Vitae*; others that the prophylactic use of condoms falls outside *Humanae Vitae*, which is concerned with marital love, and especially the virtue of chastity within marriage. Condoms, in this reading, are things, not evil in themselves; what makes them wrong is the use to which they are put; and if their purpose is prophylactic rather than contraceptive, and the purpose is to prevent infection, their use may be justified.

In *Light of the World*, Pope Benedict introduces a pastoral viewpoint, recognising that, in the case of a prostitute using a condom, this could be 'a first step in the direction of a moralisation, a first assumption of responsibility, on the way to recovering an awareness that not everything is allowed and one cannot do whatever one wants'. But he went on to repeat that condom use was neither a real nor a moral solution to AIDS, which requires a 'humanisation of sexuality'. Yet if the person recognises the other's vulnerability and so a certain responsibility to take care to avoid infection, this could be 'a first step' down that road.

The Congregation for the Doctrine of the Faith (CDF) subsequently clarified Benedict XVI's remarks. The Pope was (a) not altering or departing from either the moral teaching or the pastoral practice of the Church; (b) not referring to a case relevant to the Church's teaching on conjugal love in *Humanae Vitae* (in other words, this did not alter the doctrine on contraception; (c) not claiming that condoms are in any sense the right or moral response to AIDS; (d) not endorsing the principle of lesser evil, which is vulnerable to the error of proportionalism; (e) not claiming that the use of a condom by an HIV-infected prostitute diminishes the evil of prostitution.

What the Pope *was* saying – 'in full conformity with the moral theological tradition of the Church'– was that those who engage in promiscuous behaviour knowing themselves to be HIV-infected risk are sinning against the fifth commandment (Thou Shalt Not Kill) as well as against the sixth (Thou Shall Not Commit Adultery), and that 'anyone who uses a condom in order to diminish the risk posed to another person is intending to reduce the evil connected with his or her immoral activity'. The CDF added that 'those involved in prostitution who are HIV positive and who seek to diminish the risk of contagion by the use of a condom may be taking the first step in respecting the life of another – even if the evil of prostitution remains in all its gravity.'

Summarising these often complex ideas simply we can say: the Church urges HIV-infected and sexually promiscuous people to abstain and be faithful. The Church does not urge the use of condoms, which overall aggravates the problem. But in the extreme case of prostitutes who are unwilling or practically speaking unable to abstain, their intention to use a condom to reduce the risk of infection may be a step in the direction of taking responsibility.

Another case often raised is that of the 'sero-discordant' married couple, where one spouse is infected and the other is not, or where both are HIV-infected. The CDF's clarification pointed out that the Pope's remarks, in *Light of the World,* did not enter into that question, so it would be pointless to extrapolate. It is however obvious that in this situation a very strong risk of infection exists: the HIV-positive partner is very likely to infect the other: a doubly infected couple is likely to exacerbate the destruction of their respective immune systems by 're-infecting' each other with different strains of the virus. Abstinence, therefore, is the path of greatest responsibility. According to the II Special Session for Africa of the Synod of Bishops, the Church offers 'a pastoral support which helps couples living with an infected spouse to inform and form their consciences, so that they might choose what is right, with full responsibility for the greater good of each other, their union and their family'.

Existing frame
'The Church is more concerned with its outdated views on sex than it is in saving lives in Africa. If people were taught

*to use condoms properly, millions of lives could be saved.
The Church is heartless in its pursuit of principles over
care of the sick and dying.'*

Reframe

*The Church is the leading and often sole provider of care to
those sick and dying of HIV in Africa. No organisation
knows and understands AIDS better. The Church programmes do not just propose that which is morally right,
but also that which works best: behaviour change. The
evidence supports this approach; among populations at
large, campaigns of condom-promotion programmes have
exacerbated the problem. The Church's message seems
counter-cultural but is epidemiologically the soundest
option.*

*As Pope Benedict has made clear, among people engag-
ing in high-risk behaviour, the Church continues to propose abstinence or fidelity. If such people choose to use a
condom in order to protect another from infection, this
may well be a step in the moral direction. This is not a
change in teaching on contraception.*

Key messages

- When the Church speaks about AIDS, it does so with
  real authority. No other organisation in Africa is closer
  to AIDS sufferers. The Church knows the problem at
  first hand.
- Condoms have proven effective in reducing infection
  rates among target populations of people engaging in
  high-risk behaviours, such as prostitutes, but not

among the population at large. Campaigns pushing condoms send the opposite message to the one that needs to be given.

- Over-reliance on the promotion of condoms misses the heart of the problem. It is time to put more investment into programmes aimed at behaviour maintenance among the young (many of whom are abstinent and want to remain so until marriage) and behaviour change among the young and not-so-young.

- Programmes which deal with the underlying problem of promiscuity are the most effective of all. The Church has pioneered behaviour-change programmes which not only urge chastity and fidelity but help young people resist sexual advances of elder relatives and others, known as 'sugar daddies' and 'sugar mommies'. This has helped to reduce transmission rates substantially.

- The Church does urge prostitutes to change their lives for the better and, where possible, helps them to do so. Telling them to use, or not use, condoms is beside the point. When reform seems impossible, protection from infection seems reasonable for people already infected, or people vulnerable to infection. Using a condom to prevent infecting another may turn out to be a step in the direction of growing moral responsibility – but that does not justify the promiscuous act.

Chapter 9

Anglicans, the priesthood and the Ordinariate

Challenging questions

- *Why did the Catholic Church create the Ordinariate just at the moment when the Anglican Church was divided over women bishops?*
- *Surely the Ordinariate is a semi-detached conclave within the Catholic Church – 'not proper Catholics'?*
- *Isn't an all-male, celibate priesthood a sexist anachronism?*
- *Many Catholic priests have left the priesthood to marry. Yet the Church is accepting dozens of married priests. How do you square that?*
- *Isn't the Ordinariate a sign that Rome has given up on the idea of eventual unity with Canterbury?*

A fruitful new chapter in relations between Catholics and Anglicans opened in September 2009, when Pope Benedict XVI legislated to allow local bishops' conferences to create special structures known as 'ordinariates' for Anglicans becoming Catholics. The Personal Ordinariate of Our Lady of Walsingham, formally established in England and Wales on 14 January 2011, is the world's first, allowing hundreds of former Anglicans to worship together with their priests at special liturgies, fully part of the Catholic Church but retaining elements of their Anglican tradition. At Easter 2011, some 1,000 lay people and and around 60 clergy entered the Catholic Church in this way.

The Ordinariate threw up a number of neuralgic issues. Some Anglicans saw it as a predatory move on the part of the Vatican (*The Times* spoke of Rome 'parking its tanks on Lambeth's lawn'), taking advantage of Anglican disunity to 'poach' dissenting Anglo-Catholics. Some also questioned the Catholic Church's decades-long commitment to eventual unity between the two Churches; had Rome now given up on the idea? The issue in turn highlighted the specific areas of disagreement between the Catholic and Anglican Churches which have hardened since the early 1990s, when the Church of England voted to ordain women as priests and more recently as bishops, spotlighting the firm Catholic belief that only men may be ordained priests.

The issue also drew a line under another difference between Anglican and Catholic priests: the former, if they are married, may be ordained, while the latter, if married, may not. Why is this? And why, given the celibacy rule, is it not imposed uniformly within the Catholic Church? There are parts of the Catholic Church – Churches in communion with Rome but following their own 'eastern' rites – where married men are ordained priests. And closer to home, since the early 1990s – and again now via the Ordinariate – dozens of married Anglican priests became married Catholic priests. Why is marriage all right for some Catholic priests, but not others?

We will consider first the questions of priestly celibacy and an all-male priesthood in order to understand the Catholic tradition in each case, before moving on to the question of Catholic – Anglican unity and the place of the Ordinariate.

Positive intention

The positive intention behind criticism of the all-male priesthood is one, obviously, of gender equality. If God created men and women as being of equal worth, surely those who perform his sacraments can be either gender? The positive value of a married priesthood is marriage itself: if marriage is a good, then surely it is also good for priests?

The positive value behind the critique of theOrdinariate is that of unity. Those who desire the eventual unity of the Catholic and Anglican Churches want to do nothing that would impede progress towards that goal.

Priestly celibacy

The Orthodox Churches allow married men to be ordained priests (but not bishops). And not all Catholic priests are celibate: in Catholic Churches such as the Melkites, Syrians and Chaldeans – historic Churches of the Middle East, dating back to the apostles – married men can be ordained as deacons and priests, a centuries-old tradition. But even in these Churches bishops are always chosen from among celibate priests; a Catholic bishop may never marry, anywhere in the Church.

Priestly celibacy is not, as many people think, an invention of the medieval Church; it has been central to the Christian understanding of priesthood from the earliest centuries, even if the ideal hasn't always been lived out fully: laws 'imposing' celibacy were attempts to preserve this ancient tradition.

The Church regards celibacy as a vital, if not indispensable, element of priesthood, following the example of Jesus. The culture of Jesus' time, even more than our own, regarded marriage and offspring as a precondition of happiness and status, and those who were virgins or celibate were seen as deprived. Jesus' celibacy, therefore, was not an incidental characteristic, but a visible, deliberate sign of his indiscriminate love for all.

Just as those who chose to be – in the language of the gospels – 'eunuchs for the Kingdom of God' were regarded then as odd and unhealthy, so today, in an age marked by the thinking of Freud, priestly celibacy is considered life-denying and repressive. The clerical sex abuse scandal reinforced this idea in the minds of many, who take it for granted the sexual abuse of minors is the consequence of shutting down a sexual 'escape-valve'. (As discussed in Chapter 5, however, the statistics tell a very different story.)

The truth is exactly the opposite. Priestly celibacy, embraced as part of a vocation freely chosen, is a way of loving many with an open heart, and is a source of life-giving joy to thousands of priests across the world. That there have been many who have left the priesthood to marry does not detract from this fact, any more than the prevalence of divorce and infidelity can take away the value and joy of lifelong marriage. Both are hard; but that is what makes them worthwhile. Married people struggle with loneliness, or with chastity, or with boredom, or with a feeling that they have made the wrong decision, or with falling in love with others. These are struggles for celibate people as well as married people. The struggle is the flip side of commitment.

Some suggest that priests should be married in order to make life easier for them, as if marriage were the easy option. But marriage is a tough vocation, just as celibacy is – they are both about a lifelong commitment to love, but in different ways; and they both bring enormous joys and real difficulties. They are both 'paths to God' – vocations.

Celibacy is often spoken of solely in terms of a denial of a good. Sexual love, of course, is a good – a gift of God intended for marriage and the begetting of children. Because celibacy is the choice to live without sex and marriage, it can seem like a denial of that good. But it is a denial for a larger purpose: to enable a deeper loving and commitment. The same is true of marriage. Marriage is a denial of the opportunity to have many sexual partners. But the point of that denial is to enable and deepen the commitment between husband and wife.

The best way of reframing celibacy as a way of loving is through this comparison with marriage.

Love is sacrificial. In both cases, married love and the love that goes with priestly celibacy, it involves putting others first. Real love requires discipline. The reward is great joy and great peace; but no one pretends it's not sometimes very hard. Marriage (fidelity, monogamy, dedication to another) can be very tough; so, too, can priestly celibacy. Yet the reward is an ever-deepening capacity for love.

Catholic priests, like Jesus, choose the celibate path while being enthusiastic about marriage. Saying 'yes' to celibacy does not mean putting down or rejecting the institution of marriage. Celibate priests, are among the most fervent advocates of marriage, not just in principle but in practice. One of the priest's central tasks is to assist married couples in countless ways, preparing them for the commitment and supporting them in their trials.

Both celibacy and marriage are paths of holiness. You do not need to be celibate to be declared a saint – as shown by the many married men and women canonised by Pope John Paul II.

The difference between marriage and celibacy is one of focus. A married man, however strong his faith and his desire to serve, is called to put his wife and children first; as a celibate priest, it is the people your bishop asks you to serve whom you place at the very centre of your life. These are both vocations which require an undivided heart and a total commitment. Celibacy is about loving in a particular way; it involves a radical freedom, a radical gift of oneself, which is simply not possible if you have the commitments of marriage and family. In the same way, a husband cannot focus on his wife and children if he has many partners.

Celibacy is a gift of God – a call made to the hearts of some individuals. It is not intended for most, or even many, Catholics. Like all of God's gifts, when you accept it, it can make you very happy indeed, because you are fulfilling God's will. But it remains an option for the few, and it must be carefully discerned.

Unlike a male priesthood, priestly celibacy is not a doctrine of the Church but a discipline – which is why it can be lifted in exceptional cases, or allowed in the case of Catholic Churches with different rites. However, it is not 'merely' a discipline: it expresses a central understanding of the Catholic priesthood as a wholehearted and unconditional commitment. The discipline does not, however, apply to all clergy: deacons, for example, may be married (deacons are clergy, but not priests). While there will always be celibate priests (notably in religious orders), the mandatory celibacy rule could, in theory, be lifted in the Latin Church. Yet recent popes have re-affirmed celibacy as a gift to the Church which is to be treasured, and see mandatory celibacy as the best way of preserving that gift.

There have been many calls to lift that rule because of alarm over declining numbers of vocations. But it is the quality of vocations, not the number, which most matters. And while it is undoubtedly true that opening the priesthood to married men would increase priest numbers, it does not follow that celibacy is a significant deterrent to vocations. Where Catholic faith is strong, there are plenty of vocations to the celibate priesthood. Celibacy makes sense to young men who want to give their lives wholeheartedly; they know that loving Christ is going to involve sacrifices, and they make them out of joy and not out of pressure.

While there are areas suffering from a scarcity of vocations, it is not obvious, globally, that there is a crisis. Numbers of priests increased slightly over the years 2000–08 from 405,000 to 409,000, while students training for priesthood increased by about 6 per cent, from 110,000 to 117,000. These figures conceal regional variations, but only in Europe and Australia are priestly vocations actually falling; yet in these countries the starting-point for comparisons – the 1950s to the 1960s – was a period of exceptionally large numbers of vocations to the priesthood. And while some look back on this period as something of a 'golden age' for priestly vocations, the sexual abuse crisis has revealed how little screening of candidates took place back then; many men entered the priesthood who were unsuited to it.

That decline is beginning to reverse: the UK has its largest number of seminarians in many years: more than 200 met Pope Benedict on his UK visit in September 2010. And while the shortage of priests in some parts of Europe is acute, most European dioceses have priest – people ratios far in excess of most developing countries. What is spoken of as a famine in Spain or France would be regarded as a feast in parts of Africa or Asia.

In the case of former Anglican priests, Rome accepts that their traditions never asked them to choose between priesthood and marriage. In receiving a married Anglican into the Catholic priesthood, the Church recognises that ministry and marriage have been part of a man's life and makes a generous exception because this man has entered into ministry without realising that celibacy could be part of that.

A Catholic considering the priesthood, on the other hand, knows that there are two paths ahead of him, and he is invited to discover which is the right one. Choosing to marry excludes him from the sacramental priesthood; it does not prevent him ministering to others, being the light of Christ in the world, and becoming holy. Indeed, so much of the criticism of a celibate priesthood reflects an old-fashioned, clericalist confusion of priesthood and holiness. Priesthood is one of many paths to holiness: many holy men have been priests; many more holy men and women have not been.

Why Catholic priests are men

Because a male priesthood is not a discipline but a doctrine of the Church, the question of admitting women to the Catholic priesthood is in reality an academic one. Various popes have made clear that the choice of men as priests belongs to the deposit of faith which it is the Church's mission to uphold. The Church has declared there is no power or mechanism by which it could admit women to the priesthood; it is, in a sense, 'powerless' to do so. Pope John Paul II said in 1994 that 'the Church has no authority whatsoever to confer priestly ordination on women' and noted that this was 'to be definitively held by all the Church's faithful'. Popes do not make such declarations unless they are sure they will not in future be contradicted.

What is the Church's justification for excluding women from the priesthood? The *Catechism* points out – with plentiful scriptural references – that 'the Lord Jesus chose men (*viri*) to form the college of the twelve apostles, and the apostles did the same when they chose collaborators to succeed them in their ministry.' The college of bishops, it goes on, 'makes the college of the twelve an ever-present and ever-active reality until Christ's return. The Church recognizes herself to be bound by this choice made by the Lord himself. For this reason the ordination of women is not possible.'

Later, the *Catechism* points out that 'no one has a *right* to receive the sacrament of Holy Orders. Indeed no one claims this office for himself; he is called to it by God.' But being called is not enough; the Church must assess and verify that call. Jesus' choice of 12 men to represent him as his first priests has been understood by the Church over centuries as deliberate, significant, and applicable to every age and culture where the Church is present. That view derives from the remarkable fact that Jesus had many women among his disciples who were involved in his mission and ministry yet selected men as apostles.

Critics of the all-male priesthood point to the huge distance between women's roles in the modern world and the era of the early Church, But it is not true that female leadership is a modern idea or alien to Jesus' age. Many traditional societies have been broadly matriarchal: think of Roman matrons running the early Christian house churches, or powerful medieval abbesses ruling 'double' monasteries of men and women. Even in Jesus' time, the 'priestess' was an established part of the surrounding religious milieu. So it wasn't just a question of Jesus bowing to the conventions of his age; he demonstrated time and again that he was not bound by those conventions where they were obstacles to his mission. Yet he chose men as priests. That is why Christians in the early Church always took for granted the idea of the male priesthood. And why the teaching has been clear and consistent in every generation.

Reserving the priesthood to men is not a judgement on women's abilities or rights, any more than celibacy is a judgement on marriage, or marriage a judgement on single people. The teaching reflects the specific role of the priest in the Catholic understanding, which is to represent Jesus, to stand in his place (*in persona Christi*). Arguments about gender equality are to a large extent inappropriate, for priesthood is not a job or a position. A woman, as much as a man, can reflect the love of Jesus, and bring others to him through her faith and witness. Being a priest or bishop does not make you more holy. But the Church holds that a man stands 'in the person of Christ' as a priest, in the representation of Jesus in his humanity – a humanity that is not sexually neutral. Most Catholic women are untroubled by this Catholic understanding of the male priesthood, and do not see it as a bar to a full expression of their faith and their identities as women.

Because the question of female ordination has become enmeshed with gender politics, and because it is taken for granted by contemporary society that equal career opportunities for women represent a major historic progress, the Church can be left looking isolated in maintaining a 'gender ban'. But this is to confuse priesthood with power and career. The priesthood is not a career, but a calling to radical service of a particular kind. And while priests do have a certain kind of power – the power to celebrate sacraments – it is not power in the ordinary sense of leadership. Because women cannot be priests does not mean they cannot be leaders in the Church; and many are – running schools, abbeys, charities, church departments and, increasingly, Vatican academies and bodies.Women take a lead role in parishes, teaching, managing, organising, administering and ministering; in dioceses, women direct commissions, charities and Higher Education Institutes. In thousands of Catholic schools across the world women are the principals. Women lead church delegations, run huge institutions, and are among the key voices in Catholicism worldwide.

Women play a greater leadership role in the Church than in previous eras, because of changing mores and expectations. They are likely to play an even larger role in the future. Like any other human institution, the Church has placed obstacles in the path of women out of prejudice and patriarchy; but there is nothing in its teaching – indeed, the opposite – which gives such views succour. When Pope John Paul II chose new patron saints for Europe – rulers, prophets and academics – half were women who had a profound impact on the era they lived in: St Bridget of Sweden was a formidable mystic and leader; St Catherine of Siena publicly admonished the Pope; St Edith Stein was a leading German philosopher of the early twentieth century. The Church is not afraid of the abilities of women; it was the Church which first set up schools in Europe to educate them. And looking at the Church across the globe, it is hard not to conclude that women drive the great Catholic enterprises which witness to Christ's love for humanity.

Crisis and conversion

After years of debates, in 1992 the General Synod of the Church of England voted to ordain women. There were theological and ecclesiological arguments, of course, on both sides. But viewed from the perspective of Christian ecumenism – namely, the healing of the historical splits in Christianity between the Catholic, Orthodox and

Anglican Churches – it was an act of unilateralism which dashed long-held hopes of the Churches being united within a few generations.

Those hopes were the fruit of the initial promise of the official dialogue between the Catholic and Anglican Churches known as the Anglican Roman Catholic International Commission (ARCIC, pronounced 'Ar-kick') established in 1967 by the Archbishop of Canterbury, Michael Ramsey, and Pope Paul VI. After an initial preparatory period, there have been two 'phases': ARCIC I (1970–81) and ARCIC II (1983–2004), which have produced documents of agreement on major questions which have divided the Churches since the Reformation: the Eucharist, ordination, papal authority, salvation, the role of Mary, and so on. A third ARCIC is now underway, discussing the themes: 'the Church as communion — local and universal' and 'how in communion the local and universal Church comes to discern right ethical teaching' – precisely the questions behind the recent crisis in the Anglican Communion. Far from being an irrelevant sideshow, therefore, ARCIC continues to be an honest attempt by both Churches to grapple with the real issues which divide them.

But there's no getting away from the fact that, while ARCIC has led to warmer relations between the two Churches, unity has been blocked by very real differences between them. First, the status of the documents agreed by ARCIC remains uncertain, because synods of Anglican Churches have failed to vote on them or have rejected them, leaving open the question of who, exactly, Rome is talking to. Secondly, in the view of some Anglicans the Catholic Church has taken insufficient steps to reform the exercise of papal authority. Thirdly, the decision by the Church of England in 1992 to ordain women as priests, and more recently as bishops, has highlighted profound disagreements over the mechanisms by which doctrines can be changed. Fourthly, divisions within worldwide Anglicanism over moral and doctrinal questions have caused the 70 million-strong Anglican Communion worldwide to fragment, leading to question marks over who is representing whom. The crisis came to a head in 2004 with the consecration by the Episcopal Church in the USA of Gene Robinson, an openly gay man, as a bishop, in defiance of the Anglican primates worldwide. The crisis led to the suspension of ARCIC talks in 2005 and many years of soul-searching and debates over reform in the Anglican Church.

These four sticking-points can be boiled down into one: the ecclesiological question of authority. For many Anglo-Catholics – Anglicans who see themselves as part of the historic communion of the Catholic Church – who have hoped for eventual unity, the third and fourth have been turning-points. Many have come to realise that unity will not and cannot happen because of the decisions of General Synod. Just as the decision to ordain women triggered an exodus in the early 1990s of some 480 Anglican priests (although about 80 later crossed back) and hundreds of lay people into the Catholic Church in England and Wales, so the recent decision to ordain women bishops and the Anglican Communion crisis have led them to petition Rome for the Ordinariate.

Media reports of the those joining the Ordinariate as 'disaffected Anglicans' who are 'opposed to women priests' fail to capture their real motive; far more important for Anglicans choosing to become Catholics is precisely the question of ecclesiastical authority and communion. The view of Catholic Anglicans becoming Roman Catholics is that the Church of England has put itself outside the communion intended by Christ. It is not the question of female ordination per se which has prompted them to move, but questions of faith and order.

The Ordinariate and Catholic–Anglican relations

The Ordinariate, made possible by Pope Benedict XVI's Apostolic Constitution *Anglicanorum Coetibus* ('Groups of Anglicans') of November 2009, was the result of what he described as requests made to him 'repeatedly and insistently' by groups of Anglicans wishing 'to be received into full communion individually as well as corporately' within the Catholic Church. This was not, in other words, an opportunistic gesture by Rome, but a response to a very real need on the part of large numbers of Anglicans. As Archbishop Vincent Nichols put it, the Ordinariate was created 'out of respect for an imperative of conscience'.

The Archbishop of Canterbury does not share the views of some Anglicans that the Ordinariate is a 'predatory' act. 'If the Ordinariate helps people evaluate Anglican legacy or patrimony, well and good, I'm happy to praise God for it,' he told Vatican Radio (November 2010). 'I don't see it as an aggressive act, meant to destabilise the relations of the Churches.' He said it could be 'prophetic' in that 'here is the Roman Catholic Church saying there are ways of being Christian in the

Western Church which are not restricted by historic Roman Catholic identity – that's something we can talk about.'

The idea of the Ordinariate is that priests, religious and lay people are received together and remain together. Rather than belong to a diocese, after becoming Catholics the former Anglicans belong to an extra-territorial entity known in England and Wales as the Personal Ordinariate of Our Lady of Walsingham, which includes parishes, seminaries, priests, religious and lay faithful. Their Ordinary is not a bishop but a priest, currently a former Anglican bishop, who governs with the assistance of a Council. The members of the Ordinariate are Catholics in full communion with Rome, in much the same way as Melkite or Chaldean Catholics are; and like these, they look different from the main Latin-rite in a variety of ways – using prayers, hymns and pastoral traditions in keeping with their traditions.

The central purpose of the scheme, in the words of *Anglicanorum Coetibus*, is 'to maintain the liturgical, spiritual and pastoral traditions of the Anglican Communion within the Catholic Church, as a precious gift nourishing the faith of the members of the Ordinariate and as a treasure to be shared'.

In other words, far from a sign that Rome has given up on working towards unity, the Ordinariate is precisely intended to further the possibility of that unity – as the Archbishop of Canterbury suggested earlier. In Pope Benedict's words on his September 2010 visit to the UK, it is a 'prophetic gesture' which 'helps us to set our sights on the ultimate goal of all ecumenical activity: the restoration of full ecclesial communion in the context of which the mutual exchange of gifts from our respective spiritual patrimonies serves as an enrichment to us all.'

This is a significant point which must not be lost. The Ordinariate is expanding the borders of the Catholic Church, not creating a halfway house within it. The expansion of those borders means that Latin-rite Catholics – indeed the Church universal – now have access to the riches of the Anglican Catholic tradition, just as those formerly Anglican Catholics have gained a home in the universal Church, with all that implies. Communion is a two-way street; both traditions are richer for it.

By creating the Ordinariate, Pope Benedict is doing what popes are tasked by Jesus to do: to bring about the integration into a single family of all Christians. The Church universal, torn asunder by the schisms of history, becomes more itself – more what Christ intended it to be – to the extent that it is capable of bringing about the reintegration of the different parts of Christ's body. That process is not about asking others to shed their previous allegiances and traditions; it is about expanding the Church to absorb them. The Church is saying to the Catholics of the Ordinariate: 'Bring your gifts. We will be better for them.'

Asked to name those gifts, Archbishop Nichols in November 2010 mentioned patterns of personal devotion, spiritual reading, and a sense of mission. 'We will learn more about each other and that will serve our wider purpose of full, visible communion', he said, adding that the Ordinariate norms allowed for consultative bodies which did not currently exist in the Catholic Church. The Pope, he said, was open to the idea that Anglican traditions of church governance – for example, the next

Ordinary of the Ordinariate will be appointed by Rome from names submitted not by the papal nuncio (as happens with the bishops of dioceses) but by the Ordinariate's governing council – might 'rub off' on the Catholic Church long-term.

A list of the elements of the 'distinctive Anglican patrimony' the Ordinariate will bring to the Church might include: (1) a different approach to canon law and governance; (2) a theological tradition – as well as a family of holy people (Bunyon, Florence Nightingale); (3) the spirituality of the *Book of Common Prayer*; (4) a tradition of ministry which gives a prominent place to the lay apostolate; (5) the ordination of married clergy; (6) liturgy, hymnody and preaching.

The Ordinariate, in other words, is not simply a device for 'absorbing' Anglicans into an unchanged Catholic Church, but a means of expanding the Catholic Church's boundaries to accommodate a distinctive tradition and spirituality. By rearranging itself to integrate other Christian Churches separated by division, it is becoming more truly itself. The Ordinariate, therefore, is a means of helping to restore that unity, by bringing Anglican patrimony into the Catholic Church and helping to articulate the Catholic Church to Anglicans.

The Ordinariate is not a departure from the Vatican's commitment to 'full and visible unity' with the Anglican Church, in other words, but a practical means of achieving it.

Rome's commitment to unity with the Anglican Church has been manifest in other ways, too. The Vatican has been intensely engaged, for example, with the crisis in the Anglican Communion. The 2008 Lambeth

Conference – the four-yearly gathering of the Anglican primates worldwide – was addressed by three cardinals, and attended by a 10-strong Vatican team, more than at any previous. And the resolution adopted by that Conference, to introduce a more Catholic ecclesiology, with clearer doctrinal boundaries and a more centralised authority, have made ARCIC talks and progress tenable again. Even if women's ordination has made unity between the Churches a distant goal in practice, at a personal level Catholics and Anglicans are closer than ever in history, drawn together in a common mission. Despite their differences, they are not rivals, but fellow workers in the Lord's Vineyard. And the Ordinariate is a sign of the restoration of unity which has long been prayed for.

Existing frame

'The Catholic Church has exploited differences within the Anglican Church by the opportunistic creation of the Ordinariate, which creates a halfway house for dissenting Anglicans. The Catholic Church has demonstrated in this way its lack of commitment to eventual unity with the Anglican Church, while remaining intransigently misogynistic on the question of women's ordination, and bizarrely inconsistent on the question of priestly celibacy.'

Reframe

The Catholic priesthood remains all-male because the Church believes that this was Jesus' choice and it is powerless to change it. Priestly celibacy has been a constant tradition in the Latin Church, which is key to the Catholic understanding of priesthood as radical service to others, and is unlikely to change – although there have always been exceptions. The Catholic Church remains absolutely committed to the goal of unity with the Anglican Church, and has been thoroughly engaged with the process of reform within the Anglican Communion. Personal relations between Catholics and Anglicans are strong, even if institutionally the two Churches remain divided on key questions. The formal ARCIC dialogue has resumed, and the Ordinariate provides an historic opportunity for Catholics and Anglicans to learn more about each other.

Key messages

- Celibacy, not only for priests but for religious and lay people too, has been part of the constant tradition of the Church from the earliest times. It enables people to love others freely. For those called to it, celibacy is a source and means of life-giving love.
- Like marriage, celibacy is a vocation, a sacrifice for a greater purpose, a means of coming close to God and others through a path of commitment.
- Catholic priests have always been men, because the Church has always considered that Jesus' choice of men as apostles to represent him is significant. The Church has declared itself powerless to change what it has been entrusted with preserving.
- A male priesthood in no way implies that women are less qualified for leadership. Women are leaders in countless ways across the Catholic Church.

- The Ordinariate was created in response to requests from Anglicans who have realised that, by ordaining women as bishops and priests, the Church of England has cut itself from the communion of the Church worldwide. They want to become Catholics but to do so as congregations, and to be allowed to preserve some Anglican traditions.
- The Ordinariate is a way of Catholics and Anglicans coming closer and learning more about each other – and is a step towards eventual unity.
- The Catholic Church remains committed to unity through dialogue, and is continuing the ARCIC process begun in the late 1960s.

Part II

Chapter 10

The 10 Catholic Voices principles of good communication

Here are the principles which helped Catholic Voices develop the mindset needed for this work.

1. Look for the positive intention behind the criticism.

Rather than the arguments you are going to face, consider the value that those arguments appeal to. Look for the (sometimes buried) Christian ethic behind the value. Which other (Christian) values is the critic ignoring, or has not properly taken into account? Issues become neuralgic when they are about absolutes; clashes – like wars – happen when those absolute values appear threatened. That's what produces defensiveness and antagonism.

Rather than fall into this trap, consider the various values at stake, and how they are to be weighed against each other. Then consider how, very early in the discussion, you can appeal to the value your critic is upholding. This has a disarming effect, and frees both of you up for a calmer, considered discussion. You're no longer a warrior in a cultural battle for absolutes, but one bringing breadth and wisdom to a contentious issue.

Sometimes the value you uncover will not be a shared Christian value but one directly at odds with the Christian conception. In many of the discussions about the state and society, for example, you may find yourself up against an individualistic or utilitarian viewpoint. But the principle still applies: it's important to understand the value involved – and if you can, to name it, and show that there are underlying principles at stake.

The purpose of the positive intention exercise is to be able to distinguish between primary and secondary matters; our reasoning starts from our deep-seated values and moves to secondary considerations. Being able to distinguish the two, both in our own arguments and those of others, frees both sides up.

2. Shed light, not heat.

As people of faith we want to shed light on the difficult topics – enough heat has already been generated. But we also want to represent in ourselves and in our manner the Church we belong to and which has formed us. When we speak – as well as *how* we speak – we are offering a glimpse of what we are speaking about.

If you come to the discussion to shed light rather than heat, your emphasis will be completely different. You will be a keen listener to the other's views and opinions, however much you disagree. Your objective will be to let chinks of light into the subject, to open up the discussion, to respect their views while holding your own.

Just as you can 'catch' faith by witnessing the lives of people of faith who impress you, so you can catch 'light' in an argument. Staying calm always works.

3. People won't remember what you said as much as how you made them feel.

Intellectuals beware. Erudition is the opposite of communication, which uses simple words to explain complex ideas. It's not just about the lucidity of your arguments. It's about the effect that your words have on others.

Of course the truth of what you say matters. The purpose of being a Catholic Voice is above all to clarify. What we set out to do in responding to questions or criticisms is to shed light where there is currently darkness and confusion. But it is not *we* who persuade; it is the Truth. Our task is to serve the Truth the best we can. And we serve that Truth best when we do not try to 'defeat' those who object. Aim for civility, empathy and clarity.

Deft rhetorical manoeuvres and point-scoring can be excellent games, but they do not illuminate. A vigorous set-to debate is unlikely to alter perceptions. The danger is that you will 'win' the argument and lose the audience, whether two or (in a TV news broadcast) two million people.

Evaluate, therefore, after each exchange, according to one criterion alone: did I help others understand better the Church's teaching or positions? And how did I make everyone feel – uplifted, or battered? Inspired, or harried? Anxious to hear more, or relieved I stopped?

4. Show, don't tell.

This foundational principle of good writing applies to communication generally. People prefer stories to lectures, and are more convinced by experience than abstract argument. That doesn't mean you shouldn't use arguments – this book is full of them. But where you can, supplement them with illustrations: anecdotes from personal experience, or hypothetical situations which help people to 'imagine' what you are trying to say. Rather than tell someone that the Church assists AIDS sufferers in Africa, tell them about the hospitals and dispensaries in the remotest villages in the African countryside where nuns care for patients in ramshackle huts. Rather than say we need more hospices – which are vague, unknown institutions to most people – paint the picture of places where the dying are helped and reassured, and invite people to imagine what it would be like if we had more of them. Think of yourself not as the spokesperson of a remote corporation, but as a delighted disciple with stories and experiences to share.

5. Think in triangles.

Discussions can be very disorganised, meandering down various blind alleys until the whole theme of the discussion is lost. Make sure your contribution is concise and clear and doesn't lead anyone else off the beaten track. Hone your thoughts down to just three important points you want to make. It's very unusual for you to be able to make them all; if you can get two out of three into the discussion you'll be doing well. But it's important for you to marshal your thoughts into the three points.

See them as a triangle. Wherever you are in a discussion think how it relates to the triangle. Then bring in your point. Don't get distracted by other people into abandoning your points; don't wait for the 'right' moment to make your points; simply identify where the discussion is in relation to the points on your triangle.

Although the 'key messages' at the end of each chapter are more than three, you'll find these a useful place to identify your triangle. At least one of those points should address the positive intention behind the criticism. Having made it allows you then to proceed to the other two points.

6. Be positive.

This is a baseline communication principle, and doubly important when we are making the Church's case – as so often in contemporary society – *against* something. The Church *is against* many things, but only because it is *for* so much more – there is much it wishes to protect and enhance. Almost everything the Church says is because it wants to call people – and society generally – to fullness of life, health and sustainable prosperity. The Church is not like a grim-faced moral policeman; it is more like Mother Teresa, tending to the world's forgotten and ailing people, and it is worth holding up that image when you speak of the Church's teaching. Experience – of prayer, reflection on Scripture, and centuries of deep immersion into humanity's deepest struggles – has made the Church an 'expert in humanity'. It offers a series of signposts which highlight the wrong turnings and dead-ends on the road to human flourishing, both in the lives of individuals and in the architecture of society.

Being positive is not about having a fixed grin and being 'nice'. It is about bringing the discussion back to the positive vision the Church has for people: the endless, wonderful possibilities of our freedom. Catholic Voices should be idealists and radicals, inviting society to another, better way. Pro-lifers should sound like anti-slavery campaigners, not admonishing moralists, just as opponents of assisted dying should be campaigners for hospices on every corner. Don't be a grim reaper; be the angel that points to the brighter horizon.

7. Be compassionate.

Compassion is a quality for which Christians are meant to be famous, yet which is sadly often missing in a discussion with a Catholic. The main reason is covered above, in the positive intention section: we feel that our most treasured values are threatened. People who care passionately are often frustrated with others who appear to be dismissing or ignoring what is important to them. Yet that frustration is essentially self-centred. You are demanding that another understands and values what you regard as important. But the critic is also someone who regards what he or she believes as important, and is likely to be frustrated that you do not value that. A vicious cycle is set up.

Learning to be compassionate, even in heated exchanges, is key to breaking out of this cycle of mutual rebuke. Underneath almost all of the neuralgic issues treated in this book are deeply personal ethical questions: ones of sexuality, dying, illness, belief. It is very likely that the person you are in discussion with has had direct experience of the neuralgic issue, either personally, or witnessing at first hand; or has an experience of authority and institutions that have left them hurt. You may know that he or she has had that experience, or not; if not, you should assume it. God is a common scapegoat for anger, a lightning rod for otherwise unfocussed frustrations. Being compassionate is about understanding this anger and hurt, and relating to it, as one human being to another.

Critics of the Church are particularly sensitive to Catholics appearing robotically to repeat what they have been 'told' to think. Personal experience is opposed to institutional orthodoxy, the experience of individual victims is counterposed to the collective interest, and so on. In these contrapositions, the Catholic always comes off worse – not least because putting people before institutions is at the heart of Christianity itself. There is a prejudice that the Church operates by pumping out papal diktats hungrily consumed by people anxious to avoid thinking for themselves. But more important is the notion – we might even call it a positive intention – that it is experience that carries the greatest authority.

How to avoid appearing the cold, callous representative of a distant inhuman institution is a constant challenge for a Catholic Voice. There are many ways of stepping away from this trap: speaking from experience yourself, telling stories which also appeal to emotion, or providing counter-examples. But it may be that sometimes we simply need to be good listeners, ready to absorb the anger and hurt that some people have with the Church; that in itself is a valuable compassionate tool. If it is their first experience of being listened to by a person of faith, compassion is the most valuable witness we can offer.

8. Check your facts, but avoid robotics.

Part of good preparation is marshalling helpful facts and figures that reframe the discussion. But remember that statistics can appear abstract and inhuman, or a cover: politicians using them are usually thought to be lying. Above all avoid statistical ping-pong, which is a game people pay to stay away from. If you must use statistics, keep them simple. Make sure that your figures are to the point and clear – and expressed in human, clear language: not 30 out of a 100 people, but 'one in three'; and not '25 per cent' but 'a quarter'. Use them only when they say what needs to be said, not simply as reinforcements.

Criticisms of the Church are often based on a misquotation or lack of understanding of the complete picture. So it's important to go to the sources and see where the truth has been twisted or imperfectly grasped. Remember the bigger picture: priest numbers in England and Wales are far lower than they were 30 years ago, but still more (relative to numbers of Catholics) than almost anywhere in the world. A fact is meaningless without context and perspective.

Remember, too, that you can't say everything; time – and attention spans – are limited. Focus on what's to the point, and important. Leave less important issues for later.

9. It's not about you.

Good communication is essentially about putting the ego in the back seat. It's not *you* that the critic is failing to value or respect; it's what you represent. Your fear, self-consciousness and defensiveness are the products of your protesting ego. Think of John the Baptist, a fearless communicator; his strength came from knowing that he was the glass door through which people would come to Christ.

So let's nail this question of whether you are going to give a fantastic or dreadful performance. A certain degree of nervousness before speaking in public is inevitable. The adrenalin helps you focus. But excessive nervousness is often a sign of self-consciousness. Remember, people are not interested in what *you* think; they are interested in what you *think*.

The ego, however, tricks us into believing that *we* are the focus, which makes us alternately jittery with nerves, or puffed up with an absurd pride. If you're nervous, you might gabble, trying to get all your points out at once. Take a few breaths to calm down before you start and pause before you answer. The best way of stilling nerves, of course, is to prepare well.

Praying before entering the studio or a debate is vital: not just to calm the nerves and to put the ego in the back seat, but also to remember who and what this is for. Pray for the Holy Spirit to be with you and speaking through you. And try the Catholic Voices prayer at the end of the book.

If it does go badly, rejoice! Success has almost nothing to teach us. Ask someone you trust to go through it with you and see where you went wrong and where you could improve. This is where learning happens, and be glad of the lesson.

And remember: this is much less important than you think. And you were certainly not as bad as you thought.

You are doing God's work and trying your best. That is always enough, even if it goes badly. The ego would like to persuade us that we are either the world's greatest orator, or the most wretched creature ever to be dragged before a microphone. The truth is that we are neither, and mostly quite good. Settle for that.

10. Witnessing, not winning.

One of the journalists assigned to cover the papal trip was relaxing in a London pub after covering Benedict

XVI's second day in London. At the table next to his were two young women who were looking up without much interest at the live coverage of the Pope arriving in Hyde Park. Two articulate, passionate, young Catholic Voices were being interviewed and giving commentary, explaining, concisely and joyfully, what the Pope meant to them, to Catholics, and to the UK; and why they regarded the trip as beneficial for society as a whole. After they had finished, one young woman in the pub turned to the other and said: 'Well, I suppose they're not all crazy, then.'

The journalist told us: 'I reckon you hit a home run there.'

The power of these reactions is not something that is easy to gauge. But many people who come back to the Church after many years away, or who decide to enquire about becoming Catholic, will often cite hearing someone or seeing someone saying something that struck them, and which nagged at them.

Mostly, though, it's not the result of a dazzling argument or beautiful turn of phrase. Mostly it's a 'reframing': a prejudice or preconception is challenged, or even reversed. We call this 'conversion'. The model is St Paul, who turned from a professional persecutor of Christians to the most famous of Christ's witnesses. His conversion involved a new way of seeing. Having been scandalised by Christianity, and wanting to destroy it, he came to see that what scandalised him was none other than the Truth.

Inviting people to see the Church differently by communicating the truth about it is what Catholic Voices exists for.

In the Introduction we spoke of the way the Catholic faith 'scandalises': it causes people to react strongly and ask hard questions. We noted how a *skandalon* is an obstacle in the path. It causes people to stop and think, and question. And that can be the start of another path, one that leads, potentially, to a new way of looking at something. Or it can lead to the 'turning away' which Jesus warns of. The task of a Catholic Voice is to insert ourselves into precisely that moment, that moment of scandal when people have not yet turned away completely, but are indignant, or confused, or curious. Every challenge to us is an opportunity to witness: clarifying misunderstanding, shedding light where there is myth and confusion, demonstrating empathy and compassion and a deeper vision.

The enemy of such a witness is a desire to 'win' and 'defeat'. An attitude of rivalry and victory, of winners and losers, of 'us and them', of 'right and wrong' – this is the language of battles and sieges, of war and persecution. There are not a few Catholics who want to take up cudgels on behalf of a Pope they believe to be unfairly maligned on issues such as gay adoption or clerical sex abuse. But while they are right to want to defend him, and to put the record straight, they have to avoid being part of the same cycle of accusation and defence.

As a model, take Jesus in the Gospel of John: endlessly harried and challenged, he never falls into the attitude of a persecuted victim.

No one stands outside that cycle better than Pope Benedict himself. What did he do, after landing in Scotland? He praised Britain, gave thanks for the hospitality, kissed babies and melted hearts. He had strong words –

scandalous words – for his listeners; but they were words of reason, compassion and conviction. He did not command, but appealed. He showed compassion, empathy and real love. But because he had first witnessed, the British people were ready to listen. That was his victory, and it's the only kind we should seek.

Chapter 11

The Catholic Voices experience

In Catholic Voices we set out to do something never tried before: to connect TV and radio studios with 'ordinary' Catholics, who could speak for the Church as informed lay people. We found ourselves having to answer the question: what does a culture of apologetics look like in the twenty-first century?

We're still answering that question. But the beginning of the answer may lie in our experience in the run-up to and during the papal visit to the UK in September 2010, when a team of 23 'CVs' appeared in more than 100 radio and TV broadcasts, took part in a number of debates with critics of the visit and of the Church, and wrote a large number of articles putting the Church's case on a whole series of 'neuralgic issues'.

They were 'ordinary' Catholics – Catholics with jobs, mortgages, children – exactly the kind of Catholic you never see on TV and Radio. The purpose of the project was to connect these two worlds in the interests of both media and the Church.

The project began in early 2010 taking as its motto the vision for a Catholic laity of Blessed Cardinal Newman which Pope Benedict in September that year quoted at the Mass for his beatification:

I want a laity, not arrogant, not rash in speech, not disputatious, but men [and women] who know

> *their religion, who enter into it, who know just*
> *where they stand, who know what they hold and*
> *what they do not, who know their creed so well*
> *that they can give an account of it, who know so*
> *much of history that they can defend it. I want an*
> *intelligent, well-instructed laity [... who ...]*
> *understand how faith and reason stand to each*
> *other, what are the bases and principles of*
> *Catholicism ...*

As a result of media reports of the project in early 2010 more than 90 people applied for the speakers' training programme. Applicants from people aged 45 and above were excluded (to counterbalance the current predominance of older Catholics in the media), as were those who could not make the regular briefing sessions. We were looking for people who were regular Mass-goers, knew the Church, were comfortable in talking about any area of Catholic teaching, were not hostile to the bishops, and who were intelligent, articulate and willing to learn. We deliberately encouraged applications from 'ordinary' Catholics, that is, not people who worked for the Church or who were prominent in other ways, in order to enable the voice of the mainstream, ordinary faithful to be heard.

Afterwards, we asked them about their experiences.

Why did people put themselves forward? Here are four typical reactions:

> *'I had always been one of the faithful on the*
> *sidelines, lamenting the inadequacy of Church*
> *communications. I reckoned it would be*

hypocritical of me to continue making such harsh criticisms if I wasn't prepared to roll up my sleeves and do my bit.'

'For quite a while I had been thinking as a Church we could be doing more to share some of the insights and perspectives we have on some of the big issues we face today in the UK – issues like euthanasia and embryo stem-cell research. And our voices were getting lost in the debate, we weren't being heard and there was so much more we could give. There was also a bit of frustration that voices I'd heard in the media didn't really represent the broader Catholic Church that I knew – the ordinary Catholic in the pews.'

'Two things in particular appealed to me. The first was the project's non-clericalist vision of the Church. The Church was not conceived as simply the clergy or the hierarchy, but as the whole people of God, with the laity a vital and integral part. But the corollary of this vision is that the laity can't take the easy, lazy route of wringing their hands about the Church's plight, whingeing about the media and bashing the bishops. They, too, need to take responsibility for getting the message out. The second attractive aspect of the project was its positive view of the media. Too often, Church communications founder on the portrayal of journalists as villains and scoundrels. The media are not the enemy. They are not "out to get us". Most of them take seriously their vocation to report

honestly and fairly, to facilitate debate, and enable the national conversation.'

'It was awful to see the number of people in the media who had got hold of the wrong end of the stick. My experience of the Church is the opposite: the Church is there for us so we can be happy. The possibility to explain that was really important.'

Most of those selected for their personalities, presentation skills and Catholicity were professionals: teachers, accountants, management consultants and the like. Many were involved in church movements or organisations (Soul Food, Communion and Liberation, Opus Dei, Lay Community of St Benedict, Neo-Catechumenate, Youth 2000, pro-life organisations, etc.). Just under half were women. Very few of them had any experience at all in the media, let alone appearing on live television and radio and facing difficult questions about complicated issues. And there was an unmissable deadline: they had to be 'studio-ready' by September.

'The first worry I had is probably the one everyone has – what if I really mess this up, if I'm live on the news and I just freeze or make a complete mess of answering questions? The other worry I had was that I didn't know a lot necessarily about some topics. Having a deadline was terrifying but it also focussed the mind, knowing September was coming helped us all to crowbar the time to read the briefings into our busy schedules.'

'This was going to be something way outside my comfort zone! It wasn't so much the thought of embarrassment or public humiliation, which would be relatively fleeting. The fear, one I never quite shook off, was of letting down both the Church and the other members of the team by either unwittingly saying something unorthodox or simply using clumsy or infelicitous language.'

'My main concern was remaining on top of all the issues we would have to deal with and wondering if I would be able to articulate difficult subjects effectively. The biggest worry was the thought of drying up on air.'

For some candidates there were also professional concerns. Would their places of work understand their desire to appear in the media? Would they be willing to give them essential time off or allow them to nip in and out of work as the instant requirements of the 24-hour media world might demand?

'At work we have BBC News 24 on all the time so I thought it better the managers heard it from me rather than seeing me appear on the TV. I was a bit nervous but I was surprised how supportive they were. They made it possible for me to take quite a bit of time off which made it easier to drop everything to go and appear in a studio.'

Some of the repercussions at work were unexpected: co-workers became curious about the preparation and training and the involvement of people they knew as Catholic Voices.

'Some of them thought this was a very exciting thing and some of them thought: are you insane? You're going to be asked really difficult questions on live television on some pretty tough topics, why are you volunteering for that? It meant I could have some fantastic conversations I probably wouldn't have had otherwise about both personally for me how faith is important to me but also what it is that the Catholic Church understands on these big topics. Because one of the things that we learnt through the training is that if people are asking difficult questions, particularly if they are getting quite worked up and angry, it's usually because of something good that they care about that they feel is being threatened. If you can get to the heart of that and show what the Catholic Church teaches, you can transform the other person's view, firstly of the Church but also of the topic. Certainly I had conversations with my bosses and with other people that I never expected to have.'

Some Catholic Voices were surprised by the reaction of friends and colleagues when they discovered what was happening.

'It gave them permission to ask questions – all the things you wanted to ask a Catholic or were afraid to and never dared to.'

'Probably the most common response was one of polite bemusement, punctuated with occasional rolling of the eyes! My family and one or two

friends were extremely supportive. A few friends from the "dissenting" wing of the Church were quite scathing about "abdicating my critical faculties". On the other hand, one devout friend from a working-class background felt a bit betrayed that I was joining what he called "the Brideshead set!"

The training

Intensive briefings took place in central London every fortnight which began with Mass celebrated by Fr Stephen Wang, the Catholic Voices chaplain and Dean of Studies at the London seminary of Allen Hall. An invited expert summarised the key points, and was then 'grilled' – asked questions which the CVs themselves anticipated being asked. The briefing session was then followed by a period of 'reframing', in which the CVs identified the 'positive intentions' behind the criticism, and subsequently the key messages CVs should be putting across in a three-minute interview. The 'reframing' was then followed by role-play in which CVs were allocated different roles (as CVs, presenters, opponents etc.) and asked to pretend they were in a live interview.

'We all had a couple of sharp intakes of breath when we realised that part of the training involved five or six of you getting up in front of the others and literally being grilled live on the various topics. It's amazing how people could both feel sympathetic towards you and come up with some of the toughest, hardest, most awkward questions with a

> *smile on their face. In retrospect that was so*
> *helpful because in the end we were as tough on*
> *each other as anyone in the studio. It really gave us*
> *confidence – we were dreadful to start with but we*
> *very quickly gained an understanding of how to do*
> *this and do it well and by the time we got to studios*
> *we were ready.'*

The emphasis was on training for a short (3–4 minutes) interview and on communicating effectively, compellingly, and concisely within those constraints.

> *'As the weeks went on, we progressively got better at*
> *being able to distil the briefs down into the*
> *important core pieces of information: this is the*
> *subset of stuff that I can dip into later if I need it,*
> *but the three critical points to get across are x-y-z.'*

The training concentrated on those areas where Church and society are perceived to be at odds, and where church positions are seen as baffling or scandalous – the 'neuralgic issues' treated in this book. An essential part of the preparation was training in live studio situations with professional journalists lobbing hard questions to the CVs on a variety of topics. This not only gave them practice in the logistics of radio and television but allowed them to watch and listen to one another, and give each other feedback.

> *'I now know where to sit in a studio, how to put a*
> *mike on, what to do if the engineer comes towards*
> *me … knowing how to do that took away some of*
> *the nerves.'*

'The best part of the training was the time spent with professional journalists in the studio. It really helped to know how it would feel being interviewed both for radio and TV.'

The concentrated briefs on key neuralgic issues, as well as the grilling and role-play on the topics that were likely to come up during the papal visit, had an effect on the personal beliefs and faith of those taking part.

'If anything, the training reassured me just how positive, life-affirming and reasonable so many of the controverted teachings of the Church are. The Catholic Voices experience also forcefully reminded me of Newman's observation that arguments and reasons need to speak to the mind but through the heart.'

'The training strengthened my faith and beliefs. It gave me a sense of clarity and thinking through some of the issues added a depth to my beliefs.'

'It helped me engage with why we believe what we believe, particularly on some of the tough topics and so that chance to wrestle intellectually and spiritually with those difficult topics off the back of really high-quality input from people who were faithful Catholics and knew what they were talking about was fantastic. But also that experience where we do everything we can to get ready and be prepared but then we step out in faith and trust that God will be there and he will help us to do *what we need to do to in serving him. And there were moments – and several of us Catholic voices will say this – there were moments in interviews where you come up with a fantastic answer and you know that it's not entirely all yours …'*

Coming together

'The day when we first began to behave like a group was the day of the first media training, when it was you with these ten other people being put through their paces, you were hearing how each other sounded and you really cared about each other, you suddenly realised we're going to be doing this for real, we are Catholic Voices.'

The sense of CV as a body was encouraged by the chaplain, Fr Stephen, who celebrated Mass before each briefing session, and led the retreat at Worth Abbey in the summer. He composed a prayer (reproduced at the end of this chapter) which he invited CVs to say every day, and before going on air.

'Starting every Tuesday night with Mass made us come together as a group, as a community but also gave us moral support – we're in this together, because there's no way you can do something as awesome, in every sense of the word, on your own.'

'The spiritual aspect of the training was very important. It might seem obvious that the project should have a spiritual dimension but having Mass

> *at the start of the evening was a fantastic way of focusing our minds on what we were doing – and, more importantly, why we were doing it.'*

CVs were encouraged to pray for the whole project, to ask for the wisdom and guidance of the Holy Spirit in all they did. They were helped to look at everything with the eyes of faith: that Christ would use their gifts and strengths, if they allowed him; and that he would also use their weaknesses and failures, if they remained humble.

> *'There was a wonderful diversity within the group, yet there was a strong sense that we were working together on something that was really worthwhile.'*

Some CVs also came together in small groups, supporting one another before and during the visit through preparation and holding one another in prayer during interviews.

> *'We would get together every week for an extended preparation session and what we would do is pick one or two topics and then really kick the subject around because at that point we were all good at spotting what the difficult questions were and what made a good or weaker answer.'*

And even getting it wrong helped get it right.

> *'Small groups helped to drill down the key points, I made a flow chart and practice, practice, practice.*

> *It also helped to watch other people getting it*
> *slightly wrong and thinking: "I need to remember*
> *not to do that." '*

As the papal visit came closer, requests for interviews were beginning to come in. Many were for documentaries and specials that were being produced in anticipation of the visit that would be broadcast on the eve of his arrival. The documentary-maker Mark Dowd came to film at the one of the briefings, which would later be four minutes of his hour-long BBC2 documentary, *Benedict: Trials of a Pope*. The BBC's religious correspondent, Robert Pigott, also reported on Catholic Voices for BBC News, and a CV – the only moderate Catholic to do so – appeared on Peter Tatchell's hour-long Channel 4 anti-papal tirade, *The Trouble with the Pope*. The BBC *Sunday* programme also reported on the project, as did the news agency Reuters. 'Catholic Voices, the speakers' bureau that's been putting up sparring partners for the Church's critics, must already rank as one of the big innovations of this papal tour,' wrote the agency's religion correspondent, Tom Heneghan. 'Given the strong and mostly critical interest the media would show in the pope's visit, these speakers – journalists, lawyers, students and a few clergy – decided the Church needed a more professional operation if it was to get its message across.' The Catholic commentator John Allen of the *National Catholic Reporter* began his report on the project: 'Complaining about the church's PR operation is a favourite Catholic indoor sport, but the UK is home to one of the more creative recent efforts to do something about it.'

By this time, CV had been firmly established in the media horizon. 'Broadcasters have treated [Catholic

Voices] not so much as a kind of "professional vox pops", as a body with a well-articulated, mildly conservative opinion on almost all the central issues under discussion during the papal trip,' Robert Pigott told a meeting of BBC reporters. 'So is that justified? I think it is. The line taken by Catholic Voices tends to mirror very closely that taken by the official Church. The Archbishop of Westminster Vincent Nichols … has certainly given it his approval and support.'

> *'Another moment when the group bonded was at dinner shortly after the media training in Pizza Express when Austen said we needed someone tomorrow morning to go on BBC* Sunday Morning Live. *The media knew about us, we had our first real request, we existed and they were looking for CVs – and by the way we were the CVs!'*

Before all this kicked off, however, the CVs had the opportunity to go on retreat for four days at Worth Abbey, a Benedictine monastery in Sussex. It was an opportunity to run through logistics and give final briefings on topics not yet covered. But mostly it was a time for reflection on what we were doing: a time to recall that the whole project depended on the Lord; that we had been in some way 'called', and that it was not our skills or our abilities that would make this a success, but our openness to the spiritual gifts Our Lord always offers people in such work: faith, hope, charity and wisdom.

The papal visit

For about a month before Pope Benedict arrived, the media gave a platform to many vocal critics of the visit, seeking CVs as respondents. CVs debated with high-profile atheist, humanist and secularist critics, among them Peter Tatchell, A.C. Grayling, Geoffrey Robertson, Andrew Copson and Terry Sanderson. They had come together in a loose coalition called Protest the Pope, and were putting out press releases and statements, generating endless demand for responses from CVs.

Almost everything was criticised in advance of the visit: the state nature of the visit, its cost, the Pope's alleged unpopularity, the orderliness of the preparations, the lack of demand for tickets – all these were news stories which called for a reaction from CVs. There were breaking stories to deal with, almost daily. Once the visit began, CVs were involved in commentating on the visit for all the main news channels, and gave dozens of interviews to national and international media, and in a variety of languages.

> *'My first interview was a few months before the visit. I was responding to a major news item regarding priestly celibacy. I felt sick before the interview and breathless. As the interview progressed I relaxed into it more. Afterwards I felt quite elated as it seemed to have gone well and I didn't dry up.'*

> *'I wasn't nervous at all. The training was so good that I felt that they were not going to throw anything new at me. The BBC World Service asked me everything rather than one question and I remember thinking "that's briefing 1, that's briefing 2, that's briefing 3"!'*

'My first interview was on a Radio Scotland phone-in programme. I was a bit nervous beforehand and didn't sleep particularly well the night before the interview. Yet I wasn't utterly petrified, mainly because I had had a long chat with one of the show's producers the day before. However, the experience of the interview itself was a bit discomforting. The format was quite different to what I had been led to expect and this threw me. And to make matters worse, I felt that I really struggled to articulate what I wanted to say. In the immediate aftermath of the interview, I felt a crushing sense of frustration and disappointment – an opportunity lost. And for maybe an hour or so, I tortured myself with the remembrance of things that I should have said but didn't and of things that I should have said differently.'

The fortnight leading up to the visit and the four days of the visit itself showed that Catholic Voices itself had a clear identity in the media. Requests poured in from journalists all over the world; during the visit Catholic Voices had a headquarters in the media centre opposite Westminster Abbey, with several CVs ready to go on air at a moment's notice. CVs were present in Scotland when Pope Benedict arrived and at all the major locations of his visit, including Hyde Park and the beatification of Cardinal Newman, and cleared their diaries to ensure they were ready immediately for live broadcasts.

The CV approach is to respond to criticism or curiosity on the part of the media transparently and positively, believing in the values of journalism and the right and duty of the media to hold the Church to account. Although we are not naive about the constraints and realities of contemporary journalism – in which the need for impact often overrides balance and truth – we do not believe that the media has an 'anti-Catholic bias'. The experience of the CVs during the papal visit led them to the same conclusion.

> *'I was concerned about remaining on top of the brief, and having facts at my fingertips. In the end this was the least of my worries. My experience of interviews was that it was about condensing lots of material into very brief sound-bites. My tendency was probably to over-prepare in terms of facts and in the end it was about simple and general statements and making them in a clear way.'*

> *'My first interview felt quite hostile and I was taken aback by this. I had been briefed by BBC Wales that it would be a few general points on Cardinal Kasper and they soon launched into a whole series of questions on child abuse. It felt quite difficult at the time and as if I was under attack. Listening to it later gave me a completely different perspective, and although I was being grilled, I didn't notice the hostility that I felt when I was being interviewed. I was much happier with the end result after hearing it.'*

> *'I found that it got easier with every interview and I felt well equipped to answer the questions directed at me. Generally, I found the media to be open and*

genuinely interested in what I had to say apart from one occasion where the journalist clearly had already made his mind up and was suffering from invincible ignorance!'

'Being in a studio is not a normal thing; knowing that you are sat there being watched and listened to by a couple of million people, I don't know if that ever becomes normal. But I understand the dynamic of the media environment, I know what the journalists are looking for, that helps me answer the questions well and put across the points that we would want to have put across, so that we are well understood in the public square.'

But of course the Catholic Voices team also wanted to be part of the experience of the papal visit as pilgrims – a very different experience from being a media commentator. Some went in small groups with other CVs, others took their families or went in their parish groups as pilgrims. Sometimes they juggled both roles at the same time – moving seamlessly from pilgrim to pundit and back again.

'My abiding memories of the visit will be visual: Pope Benedict smiling gently among the children in Twickenham; with Paschal on the Piazza at Westminster Cathedral; the elderly Pontiff visiting people the same age as himself at the nursing home in Vauxhall; the lovely warmth in the embrace of the Archbishop of Canterbury at Westminster Abbey. The stand-out event for me was the Prayer Vigil in

Hyde Park, with the hauntingly beautiful performance of 'Lead Softly, Kindly Light'. And the high-point of the vigil was the exposition of the Blessed Sacrament and the image of the Holy Father knelt in prayer. Spine-tingling stuff!'

'Being at the centre of it all was fantastic. I went to Hyde Park media centre and Birmingham where I did interviews and helped translate the homily for an Italian priest. The stand-out moment was at Hyde Park seeing four huge screens with the monstrance and host and 15 minutes of silence, with all the noise of London around and this enclave of total silence. And the Pope in Westminster Hall talking about Thomas More, not attacking but speaking about the debate we have to renew in each generation.'

'It was a fantastic opportunity and a great privilege to have been chosen to be a CV. It has given me skills which will be valuable in other aspects of my life. I feel more confident about my faith and more able to articulate it effectively.'

'I think the success of the project is clear; there has been a big shift in attitude in the press, and I think public opinion, over the period of the visit. We are only a very small factor in this and I doubt actively "converted" anyone; but having a reasonable voice of normal people was important in countering the attacks and original prejudices and making it easier for people to actually listen to the Pope.'

And lastly …

The papal trip seemed to confirm the deeper mission of Catholic Voices – to help equip a new generation to put the Church's case in an era of 24-hour news. Benedict XVI seemed to be summoning us to learn how to be 'public' people, knowing how to navigate the crossroads of political and social conversation.

In 2011 the bishops of England and Wales began reaping the harvest of the papal visit by organising a series of conferences and meetings under the banner, 'A call to deeper social engagement'. It was a call for Catholics who serve society also to help shape it, to take responsibility for the architecture of our nation, to invigorate civil society and hold the state and market to greater account.

But a bridge is needed between, on the one hand, the academics, bishops and MPs, and on the other the ordinary world of the parish and the media.

Catholic Voices sees itself now in a larger role: in helping to form a generation of new Catholic leaders who can take up that call, and assume those new responsibilities. That means articulating a new spiritual humanism for our times, one that starts from the doctrine of religious freedom and Catholic Social Teaching, and brings the insights of Catholic teaching to bear on the public square.

This new 'humanism' is distinct from the secular, individualistic narratives on offer, and from the other -isms of our day (nationalism, anarchism, and so on), yet free from party political affiliation. It would be a specifically Catholic contribution to the national conversation, yet be supported by many non-Catholics and even people of no faith who would recognise in it a more authentic and popular humanism than the one currently on offer. It would unite Catholics around church teaching, and equip them with the tools to help articulate it.

If you would like to know more, please visit www.catholicvoices.org.uk.

The Catholic Voices prayer

God our Father,
Bless and guide all those involved in Catholic Voices.
Give us the gifts of the Holy Spirit that we need for this work,
especially wisdom, gentleness, courage and joy.
Help us to be faithful to Christ and to his Church,
and to be open to the questions that people bring us.
Help us to love and respect all those we meet.
Support us in our difficulties and setbacks.
May our words and the witness of our lives
give you glory and help others to be more open to you.
We make this prayer through Christ our Lord. Amen.

Our Lady, Seat of Wisdom, Pray for us.
Saint Francis de Sales, Pray for us.
Blessed Titus Brandsma, Pray for us.
Blessed Cardinal Newman, Pray for us.